# PU
## STEA

YOU are a hardy and experienced adventurer. When the wizard Vanestin summons you and offers you the chance of riches and glory, you can hardly wait! But wealth and fame are less important to the world of Titan than the success of your mission; for if you fail, the Stealer of Souls will ravage the land. The Stealer of Souls is Mordraneth, an evil Archmage who has found a magical way of unleashing all fears and nightmares upon the innocent – and even the not-so-innocent – inhabitants of Titan! This is what he is poised to do – and only YOU can stop him!

Two dice, a pencil and an eraser are all you need to embark on this thrilling adventure, which is complete with its elaborate combat system and a score sheet to record your gains and losses.

Many dangers lie ahead and your success is by no means certain. It's up to YOU to decide which route to follow, which dangers to risk and which adversaries to fight!

**Fighting Fantasy Gamebooks**

THE WARLOCK OF FIRETOP MOUNTAIN
THE CITADEL OF CHAOS
THE FOREST OF DOOM
STARSHIP TRAVELLER
CITY OF THIEVES
DEATHTRAP DUNGEON
ISLAND OF THE LIZARD KING
SCORPION SWAMP
CAVERNS OF THE SNOW WITCH
HOUSE OF HELL
TALISMAN OF DEATH
SPACE ASSASSIN
FREEWAY FIGHTER
TEMPLE OF TERROR
THE RINGS OF KETHER
SEAS OF BLOOD
APPOINTMENT WITH F.E.A.R.
REBEL PLANET
DEMONS OF THE DEEP
SWORD OF THE SAMURAI
TRIAL OF CHAMPIONS
ROBOT COMMANDO
MASKS OF MAYHEM
CREATURE OF HAVOC
BENEATH NIGHTMARE CASTLE
CRYPT OF THE SORCERER
STAR STRIDER
PHANTOMS OF FEAR
MIDNIGHT ROGUE
CHASMS OF MALICE
BATTLEBLADE WARRIOR
SLAVES OF THE ABYSS
SKY LORD
DAGGERS OF DARKNESS
ARMIES OF DEATH
PORTAL OF EVIL
VAULT OF THE VAMPIRE

Steve Jackson's SORCERY!
1. The Shamutanti Hills
2. Kharé – Cityport of Traps
3. The Seven Serpents
4. The Crown of Kings

FIGHTING FANTASY – The Role-playing Game
THE RIDDLING REAVER
OUT OF THE PIT – Fighting Fantasy Monsters
TITAN – The Fighting Fantasy World

Steve Jackson
Ian Livingstone

PRESENT

# STEALER OF SOULS

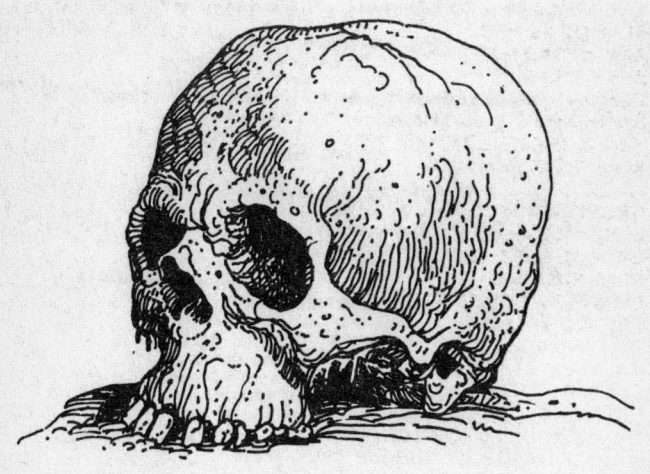

**Keith Martin**

*Illustrated by Russ Nicholson*

**Puffin Books**

PUFFIN BOOKS

Published by the Penguin Group
27 Wrights Lane, London W8 5TZ, England
Viking Penguin Inc., 40 West 23rd Street, New York, New York 10010, USA
Penguin Books Australia Ltd, Ringwood, Victoria, Australia
Penguin Books Canada Ltd, 2801 John Street, Markham, Ontario, Canada L3R 1B4
Penguin Books (NZ) Ltd, 182–190 Wairau Road, Auckland 10, New Zealand

Penguin Books Ltd, Registered Offices: Harmondsworth, Middlesex, England

First published 1988
3 5 7 9 10 8 6 4

Concept copyright © Steve Jackson and Ian Livingstone, 1988
Text copyright © Keith Martin, 1988
Illustrations copyright © Russ Nicholson, 1988
All rights reserved

Printed and bound in Great Britain by
Cox & Wyman Ltd, Reading
Filmset in 11/13pt Linotron Palatino by
Rowland Phototypesetting Ltd,
Bury St Edmunds, Suffolk, England

Except in the United States of America,
this book is sold subject to the condition
that it shall not, by way of trade or otherwise,
be lent, re-sold, hired out, or otherwise circulated
without the publisher's prior consent in any form of
binding or cover other than that in which it is
published and without a similar condition
including this condition being imposed
on the subsequent purchaser

# CONTENTS

## INTRODUCTION
7

## ADVENTURE SHEET
16

## BACKGROUND
18

## STEALER OF SOULS
23

# INTRODUCTION

Before embarking on your adventure, you must first find out your own strengths and weaknesses. You use dice to determine your initial SKILL, STAMINA and LUCK scores. On pages 16–17 there is an *Adventure Sheet* which you may use to record the details of the adventure. On it you will find boxes for recording your SKILL, STAMINA and LUCK scores.

You are advised either to record your scores on the *Adventure Sheet*, using a pencil, or to make photocopies of the page for use in this adventure.

## Skill, Stamina and Luck

Roll one die. Add 6 to this number, then enter this total in the SKILL box on the *Adventure Sheet* (your score will be between 7 and 12 inclusive).

Roll two dice. Add 12 to the number rolled, then enter this total in the STAMINA box on the *Adventure Sheet* (so your score will lie between 14 and 24).

Roll one die, add 6 to this number, then enter this total in the LUCK box on the *Adventure Sheet* (so this score will be between 7 and 12 inclusive).

For reasons that will be explained below, SKILL, STAMINA and LUCK scores change constantly during the adventure. You must keep an accurate record of these scores and the changes to them; for this reason, you are advised either to write small in the boxes or to keep an eraser handy. But never rub out your *Initial* scores. Although you may be awarded additional SKILL, STAMINA and LUCK points, these additions cannot raise any score above its *Initial* value, except on very rare occasions, and you will be instructed accordingly when this is to happen.

Your SKILL score reflects your swordsmanship and general fighting expertise; the higher the better. Your STAMINA score reflects your general constitution, your will to survive, your determination and overall fitness, and your ability to take blows in combats; the higher your STAMINA score, the longer you will be able to survive. Your LUCK score indicates how naturally lucky a person you are. Luck – and magic – are facts of life in the exciting fantasy world you are about to explore!

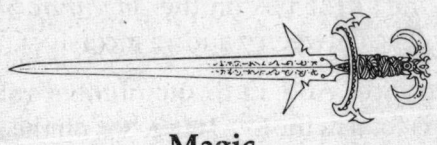

## Magic

During your adventure, you will probably find many magic items – although you may not realize at first that they are magical and you will not be certain what they do. You may also be taught to use various spells; but, to begin with, you are a warrior, and you must succeed in your great adventure by using your wits and, when necessary, your sword!

## Battles

You will often come across pages in the book which instruct you to fight a creature of some sort. An option to flee may be given, but if not – or if you choose to attack the creature anyway – you must resolve the battle as described below.

First, record the creature's SKILL and STAMINA scores in the first vacant Monster Encounter Box on your *Adventure Sheet*. The scores for each creature are given in the book each time you have an encounter. The sequence of combat is then:

1. Roll the two dice once for the creature. Add its SKILL score. This total is the creature's Attack Strength.
2. Roll the two dice once for yourself. Add your own SKILL score. This total is your Attack Strength.
3. If your Attack Strength is higher than that of the creature, you have wounded it: proceed to step 4. If the creature's Attack Strength is higher than yours, it has wounded you: proceed to step 5. If both Attack Strength totals are the same, you have avoided each other's blows: start the next Attack Round from step 1 above.
4. You have wounded the creature, so subtract 2 points from its STAMINA score. You may use your LUCK score here to do additional damage (see below, *Using Luck in Battles*). Proceed to step 6.
5. The creature has wounded you, so subtract 2

points from your own STAMINA score. Again, you may use LUCK, this time to reduce the damage the creature does to you (see below, *Using Luck in Battles*). Proceed to step 6.
6. Make the appropriate changes to either the creature's or your own STAMINA score (and to your LUCK score if you used LUCK – see below).
7. Begin the next Attack Round (repeat steps 1 to 6). This sequence continues until the STAMINA score of either you or the creature you are fighting has been reduced to zero (death).

## Fighting More Than One Creature

If you come across more than one creature in a particular encounter, the instructions on that page will tell you how to handle the battle. Sometimes you will have to fight them all together; sometimes you will fight each in turn, one after the other.

## Luck

At various times during your adventure, either in battles or when you come across situations in which you could be either Lucky or Unlucky (details of these are given on the relevant pages), you may call on your LUCK to make the outcome more favourable. But beware! Using LUCK is a risky business and if you are Unlucky, the results could be disastrous.

This procedure is known as *Testing your Luck* and

works as follows: roll two dice. If the number rolled is equal to or less than your current LUCK score, you have been Lucky and the result will go in your favour. If the number rolled is higher than your current LUCK score, you have been Unlucky and will be penalized.

Each time you *Test your Luck*, you must subtract 1 point from your current LUCK score, whether the outcome was successful or unsuccessful! Thus you will soon realize that the more you rely on your LUCK, the more risky this will become.

If things go so badly that your LUCK is reduced to 1 or zero, you will automatically be Unlucky whenever you are forced to *Test your Luck*. So, don't be too hasty or prodigal in resorting to *Testing your Luck*.

### Using Luck in Battles

On certain pages of the book you will be told to *Test your Luck* and you will then be told the consequences of your being Lucky or Unlucky. However, in battles you *always* have the *option* of using your LUCK, either to inflict a more serious wound on a creature you have just wounded or to minimize the effects of a wound that the creature has just inflicted on you.

If you have just wounded the creature you are fighting, you may *Test your Luck* as described above. If you are Lucky, you have inflicted a severe wound and may subtract an *extra* 2 points from the creature's

STAMINA score (so that you subtract a total of 4 points, rather than the usual 2). However, if you are Unlucky, the wound was a mere graze and you must restore 1 point to the creature's STAMINA score (i.e., instead of your blow causing the usual 2 points of damage, the creature's STAMINA is reduced by only 1 point).

If the creature has just wounded you, you may *Test your Luck* to try to minimize the wound. If you are Lucky, you have managed to avoid the full force of the blow and may restore 1 point of your own STAMINA (i.e., instead of the creature's blow causing 2 points of damage against your STAMINA, it is reduced by only 1 point). But if you are Unlucky, then you have taken a more serious blow and must subtract 1 *extra* STAMINA point (you have to deduct a total of 3 points from your STAMINA rather than the usual 2).

Remember: you must subtract 1 point from your current LUCK score each time you *Test your Luck*.

## Restoring Skill, Stamina and Luck

### *Skill*

Your SKILL score will not change much during the adventure. Occasionally, a page may give instructions to increase or decrease your SKILL score. A Magic Weapon may increase your SKILL; but remember that only one weapon can be used at a time

– you cannot claim two SKILL bonuses for carrying two Magic Swords! Your SKILL score cannot exceed its *Initial* value unless specifically instructed.

*Stamina and Provisions*

Your STAMINA score will change a lot during your adventure as you fight creatures and undertake arduous tasks. As you near your goal, your STAMINA score may drop dangerously low and battles may be particularly risky, so be careful!

Your backpack contains enough Provisions for ten meals. You may rest and eat at any time except when fighting, but you may eat only one meal at a time. Eating a meal restores 4 STAMINA points. When you eat a meal, add 4 points to your current STAMINA score and deduct 1 point from your Provisions on your *Adventure Sheet*. A separate Provisions Remaining Box is provided on the *Adventure Sheet* for recording details of Provisions. Remember that you have a long way to go, so use your Provisions wisely! Remember also that your STAMINA score may never exceed its *Initial* value unless you are specifically instructed.

## Luck

Your LUCK score will also change during the adventure as you *Test your Luck*; additions to your LUCK score may also be awarded after you have been especially fortunate. Details are given on the relevant pages of this book. Remember that, as with SKILL and STAMINA scores, your LUCK score may never exceed its *Initial* value unless specifically noted on a page.

## Equipment

You will start your adventure with a bare minimum of equipment, but you will find other items during your travels: there may be quite a few items, but they will fit into your backpack. You are armed with a Sword and are dressed in leather armour. You also carry a Shield. You have a backpack to hold your Provisions and any treasures or other items you may find. You also carry a lantern which you can use to light your way when necessary.

## Hints on Play

Your journey will be perilous, and you may well fail on your first attempt. Make notes and draw a map as you explore – this map will prove invaluable later on, enabling you to progress more rapidly to unexplored sections in future adventures.

Not all areas contain treasure: many will contain merely traps and creatures which you will no doubt fall foul of. You will doubtless make wrong turnings during your quest; while you may indeed progress through to your ultimate destination, it is by no means certain that you will there find what you are searching for.

Be very cautious about taking the option to *Test your Luck* unless the page tells you that you must do this! Generally, when it comes to fights you should *Test your Luck* only to keep yourself alive if a creature's blow might otherwise kill you. Don't *Test your Luck* for trying to obtain extra damage upon your enemy unless this is really necessary! LUCK points are precious!

You will quickly realize that the paragraphs make no sense if read in numerical order. It is essential that you read only those paragraphs that you are instructed to read. Reading other pages will only cause confusion and may well lessen the excitement during play.

The one true way to success in this adventure involves minimizing risk; any player, no matter how weak his or her initial dice-rolls, should be able to come through successfully to the final glory.

May the luck of the Gods go with you on the adventure ahead!

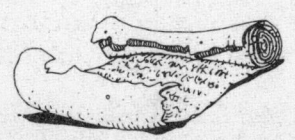

# ADVENTURE SHEET

| SKILL           | STAMINA           | LUCK           |
| --------------- | ----------------- | -------------- |
| *Initial Skill =* | *Initial Stamina =* | *Initial Luck =* |

| ITEMS OF EQUIPMENT CARRIED | TREASURE |
| --- | --- |
|  | PROVISIONS |
|  | NOTES |

# MONSTER ENCOUNTER BOXES

| | | |
|---|---|---|
| *Skill* =<br>*Stamina* = | *Skill* =<br>*Stamina* = | *Skill* =<br>*Stamina* = |
| *Skill* =<br>*Stamina* = | *Skill* =<br>*Stamina* = | *Skill* =<br>*Stamina* = |
| *Skill* =<br>*Stamina* = | *Skill* =<br>*Stamina* = | *Skill* =<br>*Stamina* = |
| *Skill* =<br>*Stamina* = | *Skill* =<br>*Stamina* = | *Skill* =<br>*Stamina* = |

# BACKGROUND

Vanestin of Pollua . . . a mage. You don't know him, but he has requested your presence, and his messengers were gracious. They had even made all the arrangements: coach fares paid, money for meals and indulgences along the way . . . whatever it is that he wants, he knows how to treat a valiant warrior. And now that you are with him, you can see from his beautiful home that he is a man of means and, surely, of power and influence. After greeting you, he has breathed simply one word to begin his proposition to you: a name . . .

. . . His origins may be unknown, but his is a name whispered in secret places, and it has come to your ears before: *Mordraneth*. Dark mage, a man of guile and cunning, one who has mastery of arcane secrets shunned by good magicians, a dealer in death and destruction who smiles as he slays. The Elves have spoken of him with fear, and you have drunk Skullbuster – that fearsome brew – with a grizzled Dwarf veteran who slapped you on the back with the only arm he had left after an encounter with Mordraneth. You weren't certain what to expect from the man who uttered his name simply to test your reaction, but you weren't expecting *this*.

You keep your reactions to yourself as he gazes at you; you take the time to study him. Vanestin is a powerful man, tall and strong, lean and still young. Not what you might have expected in a wizard! You sit in his sumptuous chamber, overlooking the harbour in Pollua, sipping his fine wine. You raise your eyebrows at the name but say nothing. Vanestin looks hard at you, and then proceeds with his story.

'You've heard of him, of course. A servant of Evil and Chaos, a mage of no mean skill, and possessed of a fiendish cunning. To defeat his purpose, we need your skill and courage. If you will accept the task I offer . . .' Now he stops pacing the room, sits down, and his voice has a keener edge to it.

'Two weeks ago, agents of Mordraneth kidnapped a wizard here, Alsander, who was occupied in magical research into Mordraneth's schemings. I last saw Alsander a few days before he disappeared, and he was excited and worried then. He warned me that Mordraneth was using magical energies to draw power in some way from the realms of the dead, and he urged me to consult with him again when he had had a little more time to study the problem. Alas, when I called upon him he was gone, with all his notes.

'But by magical scrying, we have found where Alsander is, and he is still alive. Your task is not as desperate as you may have thought when I spoke Mordraneth's name. We do not require you to slay him; we need you to bring Alsander back to us.' He pauses to offer you more wine, and he sees that you are a little disappointed – what a scalp Mordraneth's would be to boast about! Vanestin is quick to counter that.

'If you can rescue Alsander, you may gain the knowledge and power to overcome Mordraneth himself. I can't think of anyone more capable to undertake it.' You smile at his flattery. 'Interested?' He hardly needs your nod.

'Mordraneth has tried to fool us, but for once his ruse has failed. From our spies we know that the evil one is in Allansia . . . but we have also discovered that Alsander is imprisoned elsewhere. Mordraneth expects us to come for him, in the belief that he has Alsander with him. Well, we won't disappoint him. A ship has already sailed for Allansia with warriors and mages aboard. Just a diversion, of course, although we've made sure that his spies have heard of it as a serious mission. But you, my friend, will be making for the real quarry.

'Mordraneth has hidden Alsander on the Isle of Despair, a small island just off the eastern coast of the Island of Scars. Deep within the Iron Crypts he has hidden him. Why he has not slain him, I do not know – but this I do know: we need desperately to find out what Alsander had discovered, and we *must* get him back alive. And you are the warrior to do it. One brave hero can penetrate defences secretly and silently, where a group would raise too many alarms and thereby fail. And a wizard would be useless there; no magic works within the Iron Crypts save that which Mordraneth himself uses. No; it is a brave and fearless warrior we need. A small ship, the *Petrel*, is waiting.

'Will you accept this quest? If you don't, then my magic will ensure that you will remember nothing of what I have said when you leave. I cannot afford any idle gossip . . .' but he is smiling, for he has seen your hand move to your scabbard at the prospect of the adventure. 'Gold and glory, my friend, I can promise you both in abundance! Let us drink to it – but not too much. The tide will be favourable in but a few hours!'

NOW TURN OVER!

# 1

Fair weather and a good easterly breeze have sped you along your way. You should reach the Isle of Despair in but a day or two. Garaeth, the ship's captain, has been well paid, and you had no problems arranging for him to pick you up after you have completed your quest. But now dark clouds are gathering and a gale is picking up. The captain gives orders for battening down the hatches, and prepares to run before the wind. The first heavy drops of rain splatter down on the wooden deck. As you prepare to go below, a cry goes up from a crewman and your gaze follows his pointing finger; a huge black bird with a wing-span of yards – and outstretched talons – is plummeting down from the leaden sky, straight towards you! If you want to flee, turn to **55**. If you wish to stay and fight the menace, turn to **127**.

## 2

Mordraneth's magical creations can sometimes create *fear* in you; when this happens, your skill in combat will be undermined. You may use the 'Dispel Fear' spell at any time to negate all the effects fear has on you (but this will not protect you against a later attack of fear, should you be subjected to one). If you are in combat and wish to cast this spell, you can do so; however, you cannot do anything else in that Attack Round, and your opponent will score a free hit against you, doing the usual 2 points of damage. Return to **188**.

## 3

You are now fighting the young guard, who does not look very strong but who is very nimble and agile, so his speed makes him a dangerous enemy!

GUARD          SKILL 9          STAMINA 7

If you win, turn to **282**.

## 4

Beyond the east door is a dank, unlit passageway. The air is stale, and an unpleasant smell lingers in it; this gets stronger as you make your way towards the thick wooden door with iron bands which stands at the end of the passage. You listen at the door, but hear nothing. As you prepare to move in, the door opens from the other side, and before you stands the biggest Troll you've ever seen! He is HUGE, and he carries a massive club. You cannot run away, for he can easily outrun you and will strike you down from behind. You must fight him.

TROLL          SKILL 8          STAMINA 9

If you win, turn to **226**.

## 5

Your 'Speed' spell allows you to run amazingly quickly and you just escape the enclosing walls. As they crunch together, you just make it to the black passageway at the end of the chamber. Turn to **296**.

## 6

The door opens into a cluttered, filthy and reeking chamber, the lair of two Rat Men. Gleefully they grab their swords, which are stained with filth, and attack you. The smell here is so repulsive that, for the duration of this combat *only*, your SKILL score is 2 points less than normal, due to your nausea. (Do *not* change the SKILL score on your *Adventure Sheet*; this is only a temporary alteration.) Fight the Rat Men one at a time.

|                | SKILL | STAMINA |
|----------------|-------|---------|
| First RAT MAN  | 5     | 5       |
| Second RAT MAN | 5     | 6       |

If you win, turn to 57.

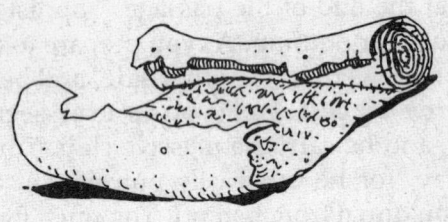

## 7

The passageway turns north and then widens before opening out into a rock-strewn chamber, into which daylight streams; you can see the clouds and sky beyond. There is a clutter of straw and twigs in the far corner of the chamber. Do you want to enter the chamber (turn to 354) or go back south and west, retracing your steps (turn to 314)?

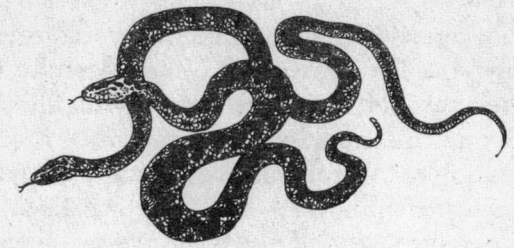

## 8

The statue crushes the gem and sprinkles gem dust on you. You gain 1 LUCK point. The statue gestures towards the stairs, ushering you upwards and onwards. You ascend to a passageway beyond. Turn to **287**.

## 9

You sleep comfortably and soundly, and you regain 2 STAMINA points. In the morning, you may either return to the trail and set off north-west (turn to **339**) or open the trapdoor and investigate what is below (turn to **157**).

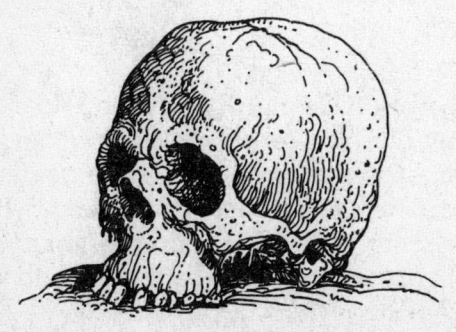

## 10

Just before mid-day you notice that the trail ahead is petering out and the hills are getting very steep indeed. This can't be the right way! Suddenly, a weird croaking voice sounds from your left: 'Greetingsssss! Have you lost your way?' You spin round to see a very large grey lizard with a yellow ruff of skin-folds around its neck, poking out its head from behind a rocky outcrop at you. Do you want to:

| | |
|---|---:|
| Attack the lizard? | Turn to 360 |
| Stay where you are and say 'hello' or something similar? | Turn to 86 |
| Run away back south? | Turn to 54 |

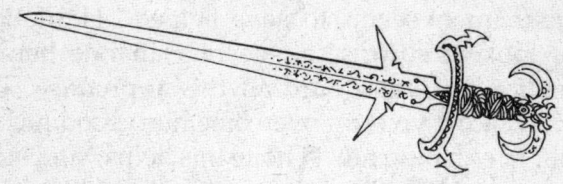

## 11

You take a swing at your enemy with your sword, galvanized by fear of what the effect of his spell might be. You don't hit him, but you do force him to duck, ruining his concentration so that his spell-casting is spoiled. Cursing you, he draws from his belt a vicious double-thonged flail with wicked strips of jagged metal studded into the thick leather! You will have to overcome him in physical combat now; turn to 321.

## 12

Obviously, whatever is in the chest must be of value, given the nature of its guardian; so you move closer to examine the chest. You try to open it; now you must *Test your Luck*. If you are Lucky, turn to **399**. If you are Unlucky, turn to **164**.

## 13

. . . You regain consciousness. Your vision slowly clears, and you realize you are lying on your stomach with someone smacking you on the back as you cough up . . . nothing! You slowly turn your head to see a thin-faced young man with piercing green eyes and wearing grey robes. 'An illusion,' he says, 'but effective. Since you believed you were drowning, getting what you thought was water out of your lungs seems to have helped.' He notices your look of surprise at meeting anyone helpful here! 'I'm Parazan, Mordraneth's apprentice. The man's mad; if you can overcome him, good luck to you. I'm escaping now! I hope this helps,' and as he disappears into thin air you notice the golden flask he has left behind. If you want to open the flask and sip its contents now, turn to **165**. If you want to keep the flask for later, add the Golden Flask to the list of Equipment Carried on your *Adventure Sheet*, and turn to **387**.

**14**

You duck behind the vegetation, and the Hobgoblins don't see you. They exchange some heavy blows, and then one runs the other through with its sword. It gloats in celebration of the kill, then moves to the cottage door. The wounded Hobgoblin manages to draw a dagger and groan, its last act being to fling the weapon and pierce the other in the back. They're both dead. Turn to **135**.

**15**

Now, will you take the light, airy passage (turn to **319**) or open some iron gates and walk down the frosty passage beyond (turn to **331**)?

## 16

At the *start* of a combat, you may cast the 'Fire Globe' spell at your opponent instead of using your sword. When you cast the spell, a small ball of orange fire will shoot from the palm of your hand and fly at your enemy, automatically hitting him and inflicting 6 points of damage. You may use this spell only in the first Attack Round of a combat. Return to **188**.

## 17

Beyond the door is a torch-lit passage which leads westwards and then bends round to the south. You notice that it is not dusty but clean, so you deduce that many people may pass along it regularly. There may be many foes here, but perhaps also someone who might be helpful if you are lucky and careful . . . Soon you come to a T-junction, and here you can either take the eastern passage (turn to **228**) or the western passage (turn to **97**).

### 18

Do you have a bunch of keys? If you do, turn to **211**. If you don't, you cannot open the securely locked door, so you decide to head off south instead; turn to **227**.

### 19

You try the Ebony Key in the lock . . . but when you turn it, it simply disappears – and the door *still* won't open! (Cross the key off your Equipment list – it is lost to you now.) Turn to **243**.

### 20

The Ogre's chamber is clean and well furnished – by ogrish standards. You take the 3 Gold Pieces from the large table (add these to your Treasure on your *Adventure Sheet*) and look around. On a smaller table by his rough straw bed the Ogre has some hard bread and cheese – a little mouldy, but edible if you pare away the hard rind. There are sufficient Provisions for two meals here, and you may take this food (add 2 to your Provisions list). There is also a pewter ale tankard on the floor which you may pick up and put in your backpack if you wish (if you do, add this to the list of Equipment Carried on your *Adventure Sheet*).

## 21

The Ogre stirs and you spin around. You didn't quite finish him off! With a dying grunt he lunges forward and presses with all his might on a panel in the stone wall before expiring. You watch, horror-struck and immobile, as a grille of VERY thick iron bars crashes down from the ceiling in the southern passage, blocking your way back. You cannot hope to bend these massive bars or squeeze between them, and pressing the panel again has no effect. Now there can be no retreat . . . cursing, you head for the other door and set off to the west. Turn to **280**.

## 21

No sooner have you won your tough fight than you hear loud voices coming from the south – more Natives, and *lots* of them! Even you cannot hope to fight a score or more of these men. You run at full speed back towards the north. This leaves you almost exhausted; deduct 4 points from your STAMINA. You have no time to stop and eat a meal so, if this loss reduces your STAMINA points to zero, then you collapse with exhaustion on the trail; the Natives catch up with you and slay you to avenge their friends. Your adventure ends here.

If you get away alive, you are back at the crossroads. Looking north, you see that the skull marking the way north is covered with blood and, as you look at it, its jaws open and blood spurts out on to the ground! Horrified, you make up your mind to head west. Turn to **181**.

## 22

You row like one possessed and get to the shore, outpacing the crab. But this takes a lot of effort, so you must deduct 2 points from your STAMINA. Turn to 102.

## 23

You cast the spell and race away. You easily outrun the squeaking horde, and very soon make it to the end of the sewer. Turn to 152.

## 24

Searching through the skulls you find nothing, but as you handle them a faint sound begins to arise: a soft moaning, like a creature in pain. Then blood starts to well up in the eye-sockets of the skulls! You step back in horror and get out of the room, slamming the door behind you to shut out the keening wails. Deduct 1 LUCK point. Now you must open one of the other doors, either the one in the north wall (turn to 377) or the one in the west wall (turn to 205).

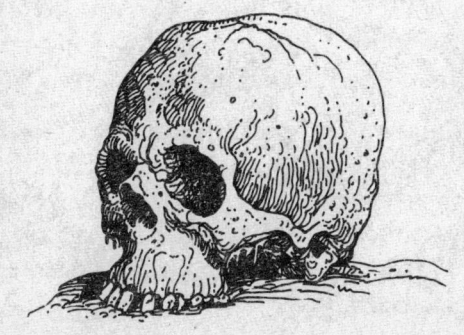

## 25

You charge into the room, to discover three Orcs sitting round a table, drinking ale and gambling with dice. The Orcs curse and draw their weapons. However, you have gained surprise over them, so you can lash out at one of them before they can strike at you. Turn to **185** to fight them – and you may subtract 2 STAMINA points from the score of the first Orc you fight because of your initial blow.

## 26

Looking around, you see that there is just one passageway from this chamber – leading south – but surely there is something useful to be found in all this debris? You sift through all the bloodied bones and feathers and find nothing of any note, then you look up at the ledge. It's a good 18 feet up, and the rock surface is very sheer. You'd have no chance of climbing this normally. Do you have a grappling iron *and* a 15-foot length of rope? If you do, turn to **162**. If you don't, you must take the south passage, so turn to **42**.

## 27

Roll one die; if the result is a 1, turn to **370**. Otherwise, turn to **344**.

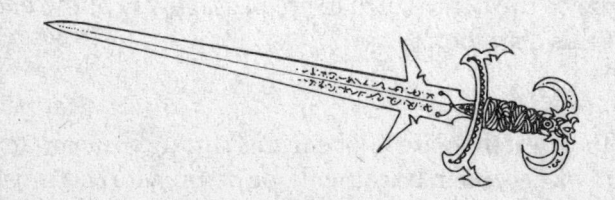

## 28

A grim sight unfolds before your eyes as you look round the door. Fierce heat radiates from a huge metal brazier filled with white-hot coals, from which a number of branding-iron handles are projecting. Tables carry brass vessels, clawed pincers and pliers; even more horrid items are scattered all round the room. You have also been seen by the room's occupant, a misshapen creature with green-brown skin and huge muscular limbs covered in wiry tufts of black hair. But he just grins at you, showing the yellowed stumps of rotten teeth, and gestures you in. You can either attack him (turn to 92) or go in and talk with him (turn to 220).

## 29

As you show the snakes the Snake Glove, they rise up and sway, and then collect together in a huge writhing spiral in the centre of the room. Slowly they wind together and form a wriggling column of scaly forms, which is transformed into a staff like the one shown on the glove! You take the staff in your hands, and as you hold it you regain 4 STAMINA points and 1 LUCK point. You know that this will drain the staff of its power, so you leave it here. Now, you may take either the azure (turn to 272) or the ochre (turn to 77) passageway at the end of this chamber.

## 30

Mordraneth's Fire Globe fizzes through the air and envelops you in burning flame before you can finish casting your own 'Fire Globe' spell! Your spellcasting is ruined, and you cannot use your 'Fire Globe' spell again. Deduct 6 points from your STAMINA. If you are still alive, you run pell-mell up the right-hand set of steps as Mordraneth prepares another spell. You can almost reach him with your sword, but not quite yet! Turn to **351**.

### 31

You cannot make it in time, and the Skeletal Illusion strikes you in the back. Lose 2 points from your STAMINA. Then your enemy appears in front of you! Turn to **397**.

### 32

You cross the long chamber, but the heat is so powerful that in places the rocks are glowing, and it drains you of strength. Deduct 3 points from your STAMINA. But at last you get to the orange passage, where it is cooler. Turn to **362**.

### 33

Since the Orc is obviously friendly, you start to talk, and ask him what he knows about torturers and any prisoners about the place. 'Yer,' he says, 'there's ole wossisface, the 'arf-ogre. Good enturrtainer, 'e is. Lessus watch sometimes. Last week we 'ad an advenchoorer in and 'e impaled 'im on barbed 'ooks.' The Orc rubs his hands with pleasure at the memory. It has already occurred to you that, if you're not careful, it could be *you* next. You decide you don't want to hear any more of this, so you set off along the passageway, westwards; turn to **97**.

## 34
Do you have an Ebony Key? If you do, turn to **386**. If you don't, turn to **171**.

## 35
Beyond the door is a narrow passage leading north, which comes to a dead end. You can either retrace your steps back through the storeroom to the main north passage (turn to **284**) or investigate the dead end (turn to **365**).

## 36
You enter the huge chamber in which stand tombs and mausoleums made of grey stone, with exquisite embellishments. You feel yourself becoming hypnotized by the singing, and you want to stay and listen to it for ever, it seems so timelessly beautiful. You could stay here for ever . . . and, hardly aware of the life-draining embraces of the wraiths that arise from the shadows to surround you, this is precisely what happens. The songs turn to screams and you hear the terrible cries of torment from tortured souls. Your mind will become part of Mordraneth's pitiless magic, and you have failed in your quest.

## 37
You don't move – but he does. The illusion melts away, so that you can see the black-robed Dark

Priest for what he is . . . but not before a spell of magical cold has wrapped you in numbing blackness. Deduct 6 points from your STAMINA. If you are still alive, he moves in to finish you off with his mace. Turn to **367**.

### 38

The trail splits; you can either head north, where you can see hilly terrain and bracken in the distance (turn to **238**), or you can continue west along what appears to be a fairly well-used mud track (turn to **349**).

### 39

The Sprite thanks you for your mercy; in return for sparing his life he gives you a small pouch with three tiny bags of 'Luck Powder'. Add these to the list of Equipment Carried on your *Adventure Sheet*. Each of these bags contains a sprinkling of magical dust which, if shaken on your hands, will restore 1 LUCK point. You may use this magic to restore lost LUCK points at any time except during a combat. Shame-facedly, the Sprite promises not to disturb you again.

You wake next morning fairly refreshed by your sleep and regain 2 STAMINA points. Turn to **103**.

### 40

Trying to bend the iron railings is a very hard test of your abilities. Roll two dice and add 3 to the number you roll. If the total is less than or equal to your current SKILL score, then you have succeeded in bending the bars apart and you can squeeze through them (turn to 326). If the total is greater than your current SKILL score, turn to 312.

## 41

The Orcs admire the bone dice. 'Luvverly bit uv work,' one of them says as he gulps down another pint of Brain Damage. 'Fancy a little gamble then?' If you have some Treasure and are willing to gamble on a dice game, turn to 291. If you have no Treasure, or are unwilling to gamble, turn to 180.

## 42

You head south, back to an east-west passageway. To the east, a pall of black smoke blocks your path. The choking fumes make that way impassable, so you must head west and then follow that passageway as it bends southwards. Turn to 218.

## 43

The sleeper is now fully awake. Irrespective of what you say, he looks at you with deep suspicion, and says, 'You're not one of us! I know all the Master's men!' He draws his sword; you're going to have to fight him.

GUARD          SKILL 6          STAMINA 8

If you win, turn to 357.

## 44

Having overcome your formidable enemy, you take some keys from his belt and release the prisoner from the cell in which he is being kept; from the darkened cell, full of filthy straw and lice, you lead a weak old man, his white hair and beard streaked with dirt. If you have any Provisions or a magical 'potion of healing', you *must* give him one or the other now, for you have a feeling that his magic will increase your chances of escape from here, and he will need all his strength to use it. He thanks you for your kindness. Turn to 140.

## 45

Do you have a crowbar? If you do, turn to 141. If you don't, turn to 396.

## 46

At last you are fighting with your sword against the evil Arch-mage! But he is swift and deadly as a warrior too, and uses his sword well. His green eyes glitter in the flaring light of the smouldering braziers as he attempts to slay you. Will you triumph or be slain at the last?

MORDRANETH      SKILL 10     STAMINA 17

If you win, turn to **400**.

### 47

Your magical Ring of Fire Resistance minimizes the damage you take, so you have to deduct only 1 STAMINA point. You're nearly half-way up, but you can see your enemy preparing another attack! Turn to **351**.

### 48

What will you use against the rats? Will you get out:

| | |
|---|---:|
| A white gem? | Turn to **317** |
| A block of incense? | Turn to **64** |
| A silver feather? | Turn to **232** |
| An ivory statuette? | Turn to **93** |

### 49

You reckon that you can pry open the lid of the chest with a crowbar – but, as you jam the hook of the crowbar under the lid and make your first attempt, the resistance of the chest is terrific. You can be sure that it will take a great deal of strength, and some STAMINA loss, to get this chest open – and you cannot even be certain of success. You can try again to open it (turn to **316**) or give up the attempt, return to the main passage, and open the door at the southern end of it (turn to **124**).

## 50

In the room beyond the small door you quickly spot a trapdoor in the floor which is half covered by a tatty rug, and heavily barred from your side. The room is sparsely furnished: a bed with clean bedding, a chair and a table on which stands a small portable incense-burner. Do you have any blocks of incense? If you do, turn to **234**. If you don't, turn to **305**.

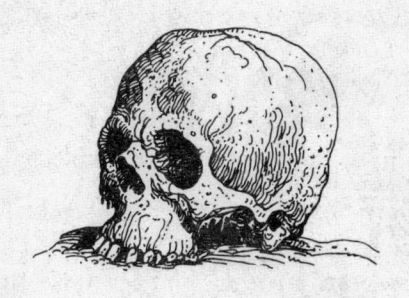

## 51

The passageway winds on to the west and seems to come to a dead end – but you can make out faint rays of daylight through the wall at the end of it! Clearly, someone slipped up when installing this illusion here! Cautiously you poke at the wall, and find that you can step through it safely. As you do, you see that there is a passageway going south which you could take (if you do, turn to **42**); alternatively, you could follow a narrow passageway that goes north into a daylight-filled chamber, from which you can hear a low cawing noise and the sound of something being horribly ripped apart (turn to **385**).

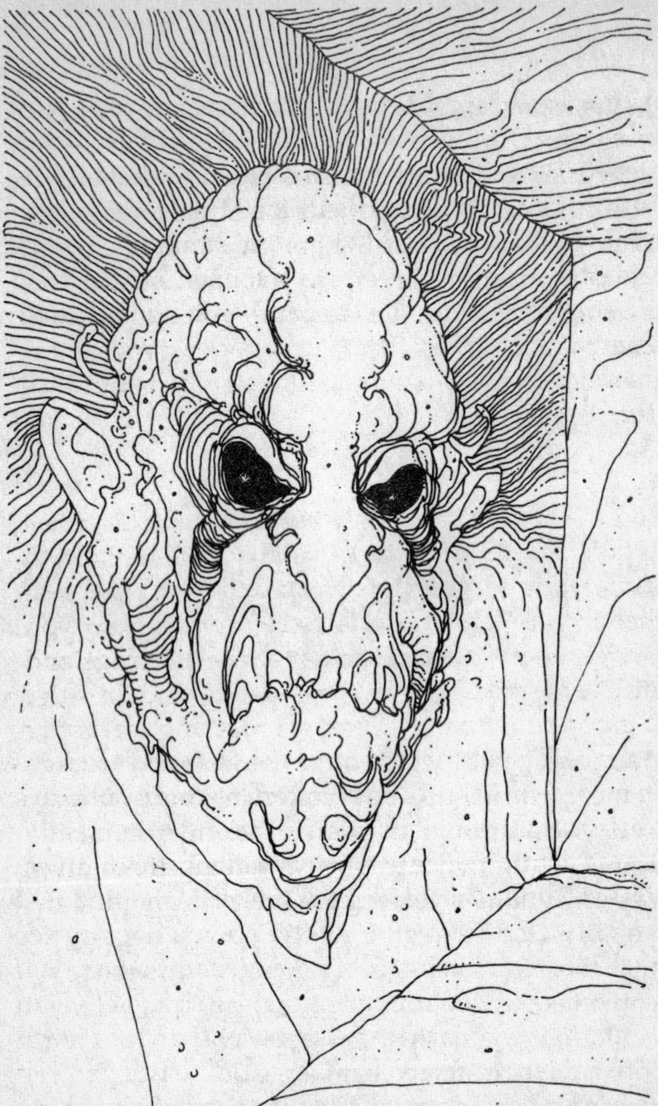

## 52

As you enter, an unexpected event makes you jump in alarm. On the west wall of the chamber is an etched stone face, a hideous and gnarled visage with cruel fangs. Your medallion flares briefly with white light; the closed eyes of the stone face open, and smooth jet-black eyes turn to look at you! This experience makes you feel like getting out fast; fortunately, you can try a door in the east wall of this chamber (turn to **313**) or another in the south wall (turn to **121**).

## 53

You make good progress, but eventually it grows dark, and you know there will be no moonlight to guide you, so you must stop and rest. The best shelter you can find is a rock overhang; so you bivouac there, after collecting a few dry twigs and the like to spread around your resting place in order to give you warning of any approaching marauder in the night. Nothing disturbs you, but you manage no more than a fitful doze. Still feeling rather weary, you arise at dawn as the first rays of sunshine stretch across the pale blue, cloudless sky to greet you, and you set off along the trail once more. Turn to **339**.

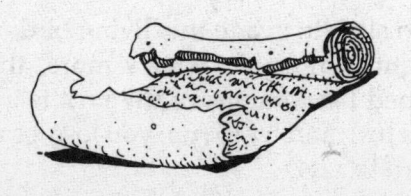

**54**
Running quickly back towards the south, you reach the turning to your right and head west along it; but you are very tired from running so fast and must deduct 2 STAMINA points. Turn to **349**.

**55**
You are too slow to evade the diving bird; you will have to fight it after all. What's more, the sharp yellow-tipped black talons of the bird tear at your back as you turn and try to run; you lose 2 STAMINA points. Turn to **127**.

## 56

'I do not know of such a place,' he says sadly, 'but I believe there is some kind of evil shrine to the south-west. Perhaps this is what you seek.' Now you may either ask him about the scroll, if you have it (turn to **302**), or take your leave and head off southwards (turn to **250**).

## 57

The Rat Men's room is quite disgustingly dirty and littered with debris; you can see nothing of obvious value or interest lying around here. Nor are there any doors or passages leading from the room, save for the one you entered by. If you wish to make a thorough search of the room, turn to **259**. If you prefer to get out now and head back southwards, turn to **303**.

## 58

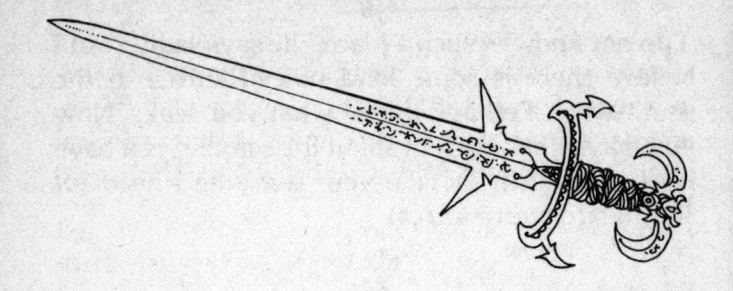

The stairs continue upwards for some distance, and time passes as you slog on, so you must eat a meal here. You are growing weary from your exertions, and you know that soon you should find somewhere safe to rest and sleep. But you can hardly do this on the stairs! Your footfalls echo gently on the stone steps, and strange whisperings and chitterings flit among the ghostly cobwebs on the mould-streaked walls. You must have a light source to move safely up the stairs (your lantern, or a Magic Sword if you have one).

At last you reach a landing at the top of the stairs. There is a rotten-looking wooden stepladder standing here, covered in mould, and in the ceiling you see a wooden trapdoor. You look around, but there is no other way out, and going back down the stairs is pointless. Gingerly you ascend the ladder. You're going to have to open the trapdoor, so you summon up all your strength and push hard. Roll one die. If the score is 1 or 2, turn to **265**. If the score is 3 or higher, turn to **375**.

## 59

You enter a gloomy, dirty and rather small room in which two bored Orcs are sitting at a table gnawing at a roast Dwarf joint. They look cruel and mean, and have their swords ready to hand. They attack at once; in the doorway, you can fight them one at a time.

|            | SKILL | STAMINA |
|------------|-------|---------|
| First ORC  | 5     | 4       |
| Second ORC | 5     | 6       |

If you win, turn to **264**.

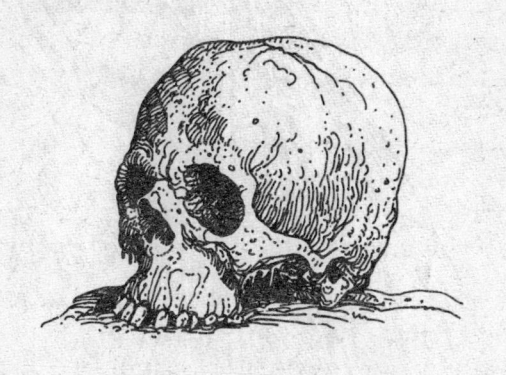

## 60

The young man laughs with incredulity. 'Oh yeah? And I'm a goblin's granny!' Before you can react, he nicks your arm with his dagger. Lose 2 STAMINA points. Now you must fight him, so turn to **3**.

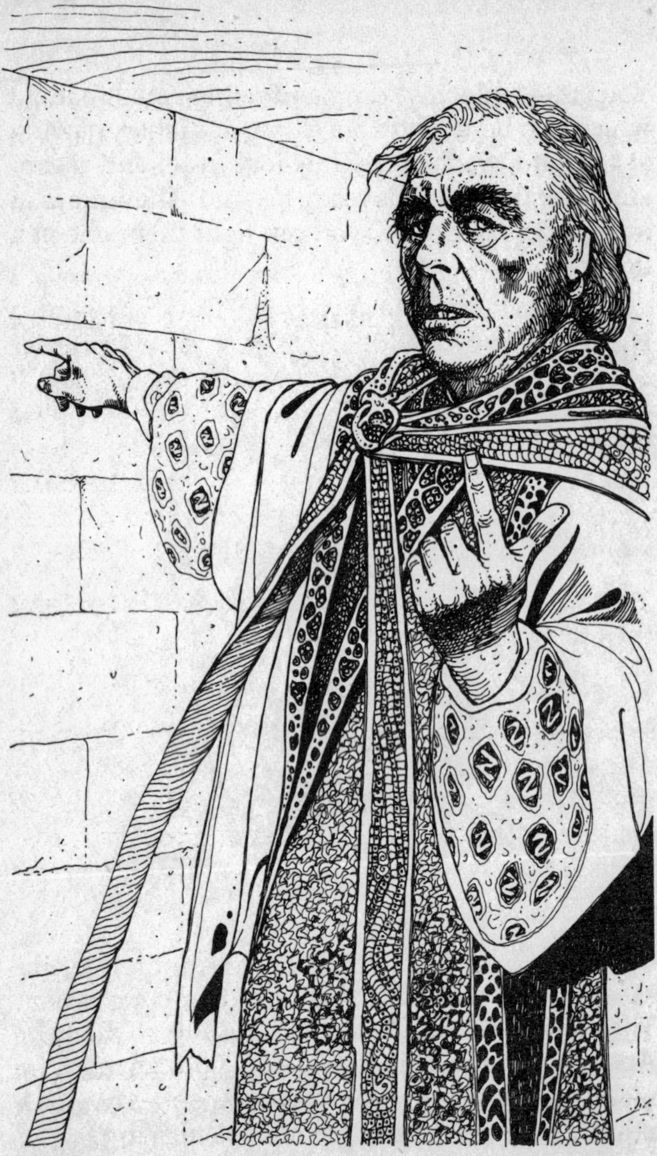

## 61

Alsander looks weary and pale after teaching you his spells. 'I have just enough strength to teleport home,' he whispers. 'Oh, I nearly forgot . . . how to get to the Empire of Illusions. There's a secret door over there,' and he points to the centre of the south wall. 'Go through it and follow the passageway. I must warn you: there are two evil Dark Elves down there, and beyond their lair is a teleport device which will take you to Mordraneth's deepest lair. If you can slay him, the illusions will disappear, and you'll be able to find a way out. Use the magic I have taught you wisely, for you can use each spell but once!' Then he murmurs a few words, and his body shimmers and is gone, teleported back to Pollua.

You make your preparations and set off to confront the Dark Elves. Turn to **281**.

## 62

You drag yourself up on to the plateau. Crawling across the rock to stay out of the howling wind, you finally reach a brown passage, and at last you can stand up, dust yourself off, and press onwards. Turn to **247**.

## 63

You race up the stone steps, but Mordraneth is able to attack you with a spell before you can get to him. You see a ball of fire shooting towards you, leaving a thin plume of black smoke hanging in the air. Are you wearing a bronze ring? If you are, turn to **126**. If you aren't, turn to **190**.

## 64

The incense makes no difference to the swarming rats. Deduct 1 STAMINA point through wasting time retrieving the item while the rat-pack was biting; now you realize your mistake and run away. Turn to **251**.

## 65

Now, you can either search the scattered piles of debris in this room (turn to **343**) or leave this place and set off west along the passageway (turn to **97**).

## 66

The cowled figure sprays a volley of blue whirling icy darts from his fingers and they fly through the air at you. Roll one die and add 1 to the total; this number is the number of STAMINA points you lose as these icy, numbing missiles strike you. Now the evil figure whirls a vicious metal-studded black flail to finish you off with. Turn to **321**.

## 67

Do you have a silver feather? If you do, and you want to offer it to him, turn to **83**. If you want to offer some other item, turn to **235**.

## 68

You dodge past the statue and race up the stairs. Behind you, you hear no sounds of the statue following you. You breathe a sigh of relief and ascend to the passageway beyond. Turn to **287**.

## 69

As you attack, the illusion vanishes! The man, no longer in chains, is clad in dark flowing robes and he wields a heavy ebony mace. You are in combat with a fearsome enemy, a Dark Priest! Turn to **367**.

## 70

You beach your boat – but hardly are you out of the water on to the pebbled shore when an angry giant comes rushing at you from the north. His massive muscles are knotted with rage, and his fists – the size of hams – clutch a massive oaken club. 'You killed Edwina!' he roars, and you realize he must be referring to his pet crab. There is a trail to the west, but the giant is already upon you: you're going to have to fight him. Turn to **240**.

## 71

The old man is barely conscious and is clearly very weak; his lips are cracked and dry and his skin is ashen. You give him some food and water to revive him; subtract 1 from your Provisions list. Slowly he gains strength and at last is able to speak. He tells you that he is a herbalist who has come to the island seeking rare medicinal herbs. The two Hobgoblins had captured him and were arguing over which of them was to kill him! He thanks you for your help, but says that there is little he can do in return, since the Hobgoblins ate his food and burned all his herbs. But he would like to help if he can. Will you:

| Ask him the way to the Iron Crypts? | Turn to 56 |
| Ask him about the scroll (if you have it)? | Turn to 302 |
| Take your leave and retrace your steps towards the south? | Turn to 250 |

**72**

Following the passage east, you ignore a turning to the south which you know only leads back to the goblin room, and you press on eastwards. Turn to **160**.

**73**

You slay the Orcs, then look around their room; save for them and their inferior weapons and the dice and coins on the table, there does not seem to be much here. Will you:

| Open the north door? | Turn to 346 |
| Open the east door? | Turn to 4 |
| Search the room? | Turn to 137 |

**74**

None of the many keys on the bunch you took from the Troll will fit the door and you just can't open it! Will you now:

| Try using the phial of White Oil, if you have it? | Turn to 138 |
| Give up and try the west door? | Turn to 358 |
| Give up and go south? | Turn to 283 |

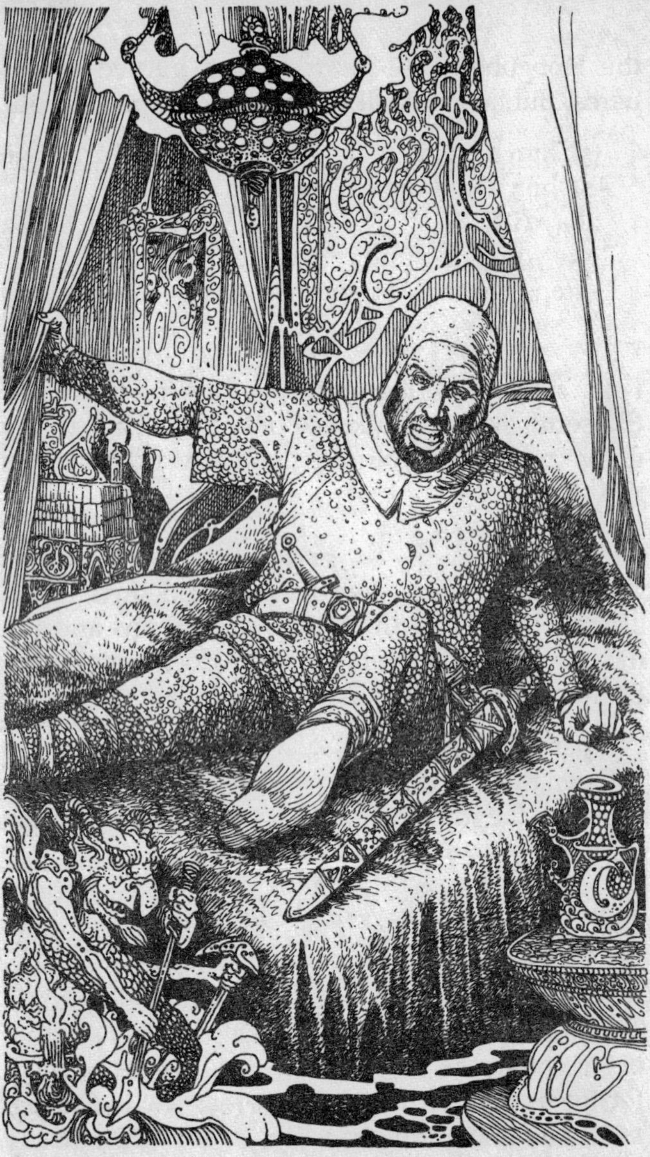

## 75

You enter a well-furnished room with carpets, paintings and fine ornaments, lit by ornate oil-lamps. On a fur-covered bed lies a man who is wearing chain-mail and has a scabbarded sword at his belt; he was obviously sleeping, but your entry has awakened him. Turn to **43**.

## 76

You are now fighting a wily, strong half-Ogre! He advances on you brandishing a heated iron from the brazier, and you will need all your skill to beat him!

| HALF-OGRE TORTURER | SKILL 8 | STAMINA 14 |

If you win, turn to **273**.

## 77

The ochre passage has a rocky floor, and the air is dry and warm. You walk along carefully, in order to avoid stubbing your toes on the rocks which are scattered over the ground. You enter a long, narrow ochre chamber. At the far end of it you see a dark tunnel in which flares and gouts of red light flicker from time to time. You head towards this, but you are only half-way across the chamber when you hear a loud crunching sound, as if of moving stone. The walls are moving in to crush you! You see that even if you run flat out, you will be desperately fortunate to make the dark passageway in the distance before you are crushed to death. Will you:

| Cast a spell? | Turn to **372** |
| Use an item from your backpack? | Turn to **45** |
| Run as fast as you can and hope? | Turn to **396** |

## 78

Before you can complete the casting of your spell, Mordraneth's own spell hits you; a ball of lightning, blue and sparking, fizzes through the air and hammers into your chest. Deduct 4 STAMINA points; also your own spellcasting is ruined; and you cannot use your spell again. Now, assuming you are still alive, you can take either the left-hand set of steps to the balcony (turn to **332**) or the right-hand set of steps up (turn to **63**).

## 79

As the whirling magical bolus whistles through the air towards you, your silver ring seems to absorb it into itself. The ring, which felt so dead and lifeless, must be able to absorb at least some kinds of magic – and may have just saved your life! Now you race to the top of the steps and you can fight the wizard. Turn to **46**.

## 80

You cannot fight the rat-pack; there are simply far too many of them. Deduct 1 point from your STAMINA, and then you must flee down the sewer. Turn to **251**.

## 81

Do you have a crowbar? If you do, turn to **49**. If you don't, turn to **233**.

## 82

Beyond the door is a dark room, with satins and silks draped over a long table. Crossed knives with sharp, serrated blades decorate the walls, together with pinioned skulls. A powerful emanation of evil radiates from here, and you feel the hairs standing up on the nape of your neck; lose 1 LUCK point. You want to get away, so you open the door to the east in the Orc's room; turn to **123**.

## 83

The Birdman takes the silver feather with a strange, cawing cry of joy and puts it on a silver chain round his neck (cross the silver feather off the list of Equipment Carried on your *Adventure Sheet*). The Birdman has trouble speaking your language, but eventually you learn much from his stumbling words.

He tells you that an intense magical evil in the Iron Crypts is driving his people out of the mountain; but this feather – a magic which the Birdmen know how to use – will protect them. He says that the 'evil ones' have a prisoner deep within the Iron Crypts, and that there is a half-ogre torturer there also. Lastly, he warns you that there is a vicious predator to the west which has just taken up residence: a Razorbeak Bird. The Birdman knows that this bird has stolen a magical item from a wizard recently, and that this might be helpful to you, but you'll have to kill the bird to get it – and that won't be easy! Thanking you for your gift, he flies off to join his fellows. Turn to **292**.

## 84

You are fighting a Stone Golem. It strikes at you with its hard stone fists, and it is not easy to parry or strike successfully with an ordinary sword. When you succeed in hitting your adversary, you must roll one die; on a roll of 1 or 2, your blow is ineffective and does no damage to the Golem.

STONE GOLEM       SKILL 8       STAMINA 11

If you win, you take the stairs up past the shattered Golem; turn to **287**.

## 85

You become confused as you travel along. You are lost, increasingly tired, and you must sit down and eat another meal or lose all but 1 STAMINA point. As you lean back against the rough wall for support, a pair of stone claws encircle your arms! You have fallen into the clutches of the Stone Shapeshifter, an ancient and evil rock-being which preys on those who wander in these subterranean realms. Your scream of horror is smothered as a wet stone protuberance wraps around your face, and you are slowly absorbed into the stone wall. Your quest ends here, for the Stone Shapeshifter's evil patience has been rewarded once again.

## 86

The strange talking lizard seems friendly, and it wants your help. It tells you that a foul pair of predators, Giant Stormbirds, are in the habit of stealing its eggs. The lizard can't climb up to the birds' nest to drive them away. It wants you to kill the birds for it, and it promises you a reward – a fine rosy-pink pearl! Will you:

| | |
|---|---|
| Say you've already killed one Stormbird? | Turn to **378** |
| Agree to help the lizard? | Turn to **256** |
| Refuse to help? | Turn to **119** |

## 87

As you rush to the attack, the Hobgoblins forget their differences and turn to attack you! You must fight both of them *together*. Roll two dice and add your SKILL score; then roll two dice for each of the Hobgoblins every Attack Round and add their SKILL scores. The combatant with the highest Attack Strength is the one who will get in a successful strike during that Attack Round.

| | SKILL | STAMINA |
|---|---|---|
| First HOBGOBLIN | 5 | 6 |
| Second HOBGOBLIN | 6 | 7 |

If you win, turn to **135**.

## 88

After a cursory look around, the Goblin departs. You wait for an hour, then another, then a third . . . but nothing happens. You really should have tried to lure the Goblin out! Now you will have to make your way out of the catacombs and back overland to the main trail leading north, and during this time you must eat *two* meals (make the necessary deduction from your Provisions on your *Adventure Sheet*). Turn to 53.

## 89

You win at the gambling game; roll one die: this is the number of Gold Pieces you win from the Orcs. Add your winnings to your Treasure on your *Adventure Sheet*. The Orcs drown their sorrows in more of their foul beer; you take care to drink only a very little! Turn to 254.

## 90

The lock and hinges on this door are very rusty, and the door looks very solid. Will you:

| | |
|---|---|
| Try smashing down the door? | Turn to 210 |
| Try using an Ebony Key to open the door? | Turn to 275 |
| Try using the bunch of keys to open the door? | Turn to 74 |
| Try using the phial of White Oil to lubricate the lock and/or hinges of the door? | Turn to 138 |
| Give up and try the west door? | Turn to 358 |

Give up and head south down
the passage? Turn to **283**

### 91

Although there are valuables here – the carpets and furs – you can hardly carry them around with you. However, there are two other items of value. First, while the warrior's sword is inferior to your own, his chain-mail armour is certainly better than your leather armour! You can put this on (add it to the list of Equipment Carried on your *Adventure Sheet*), and it will add 1 point of SKILL to your total. This addition *will* grant you a higher SKILL score than your *Initial* level – *unless that Initial level was 11 or 12* (you're so good it won't make any difference!). You also find a crowbar, and you may take this if you wish (if you do, add it to the list of Equipment Carried on your *Adventure Sheet*). You leave this room and try the southern door in the next room; turn to **245**.

### 92

You are now fighting a wily and strong half-Ogre! He advances on you wielding a barbed metal rod mounted on a short wooden pole-arm, and he is no mean opponent!

HALF-OGRE
TORTURER       SKILL 8       STAMINA 14

If you win, turn to **44**.

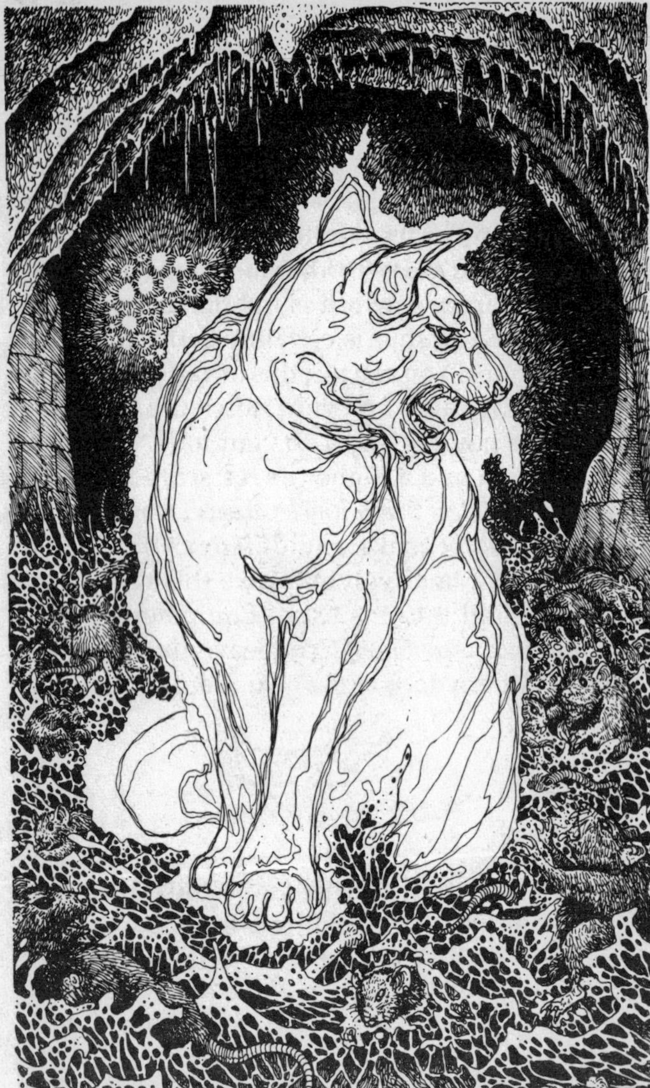

## 93

As you produce the ivory cat statuette, it seems to glow and grow in size. The rats shrink back. It gets bigger and bigger, and the rats begin to flee, squeaking in terror, as a huge spectral cat chases them back down the sewer! You continue your journey without being troubled; turn to **152**.

## 94

You are in a spell combat with Mordraneth, for you are both casting 'Fire Globe' spells at each other! You must first roll two dice for each of you, then add your respective SKILL scores (Mordraneth's SKILL is 10), to determine who has the higher Attack Strength for this Attack Round. If you have the higher Attack Strength, turn to **222**. If Mordraneth has the higher Attack Strength, turn to **174**.

## 95

As the skeletal figure approaches, your medallion shines brightly; you take a swing at the figure with your sword – and it disappears into wisps of smoke, struck by your sword and the glittering white light cast by the medallion! But now the medallion grows dim and dull, and you suspect its powers are exhausted. Now, you can either follow the blue passageway (turn to **261**) or the violet passageway (turn to **150**).

## 96

You look around and pick up the 8 Gold Pieces the Dark Elves had (add this to your Treasure on your *Adventure Sheet*), but beside this you see a better treasure still. Wrapped in large moist broadleaf wrappings are six small flat loaves of sweet wheybread – each one equivalent to a full meal! You may add 6 to your Provisions list on your *Adventure Sheet* for these. The rich smell of spices, the glitter of silks and other treasures do not tempt you, for you cannot carry these items. To the east of the room, you see an archway leading to a small circular chamber and you approach to look at it. In the centre is a raised podium on which a swirl of rainbow colours eddies and flows . . . the teleport device Alsander told you of! Breathing in deeply, you step into the waves of light, and the room fades from your sight. Where will you arrive? To find out, turn to **229**.

## 97

The passageway goes on westwards, and then turns south again; once more it is clear that you are treading a well-frequented path. At the end of the passage you observe a wooden door with a handle bearing an ornate door-plaque of bronze and a silvered door-handle. Just before this, there is a side-passage to the east, at the end of which is a small door which has a sign affixed to it: 'DANGER! KEEP OUT!' Do you want to open the southern door at the end of the corridor (turn to **124**) or investigate the east door at the end of the side-passage (turn to **172**)?

## 98

You can see an obvious and definitely *not* concealed door at the end of the corridor – but you now also find a concealed door in the west wall of the passage, about ten yards away from it. Cautiously you open the secret door and pass along the narrow tunnel beyond. This tunnel is very dark, and you will need a light source to see by. It is dusty and damp, and the air is very stale. The tunnel winds to the west, then southwards, and then turns east again to an apparent dead end; you guess that there must be another secret door at the end of it. You burst through that door, which opens into the west wall of a room beyond. There are two Orcs in this room, sitting at a table and eating a joint of roast Dwarf; with the benefit of surprise, however, you slay one before he can even get up! Turn to **59**, and fight the second Orc there *only*.

## 99

You search the Orc's room, but find only empty crates and some packing, a bed and a table and a pair of rickety chairs. However, in one crate you do find a 15-foot length of rope, and you may take this if you wish (if you do, add it to the list of Equipment Carried on your *Adventure Sheet*). Looking around, you see that there is only one exit, a door in the north wall, so you open it and move along the passage beyond. After a few yards you find that you can either continue on north (turn to **284**) or investigate a door at the end of a small side-passage to the east (turn to **304**).

## 100

Before you, in the south passage, stands a skeletal figure armed with a thonged flail! The Skeleton Man advances on you, so you will have to fight him.

SKELETON MAN     SKILL 8     STAMINA 6

If you win, turn to **241**.

## 101

In the morning, before departing you can ask Alkandi about the Message Scroll, if you have it. If you wish to do this, turn to the paragraph with the same number as that written on the scroll. As you are about to leave, the shaman tells you not to turn north when you get back to the crossroads, for his people have seen dangerous Hobgoblins in that direction. You thank him for his advice (add 1 LUCK point). You take your leave and head north to the crossroads (turn to **181**).

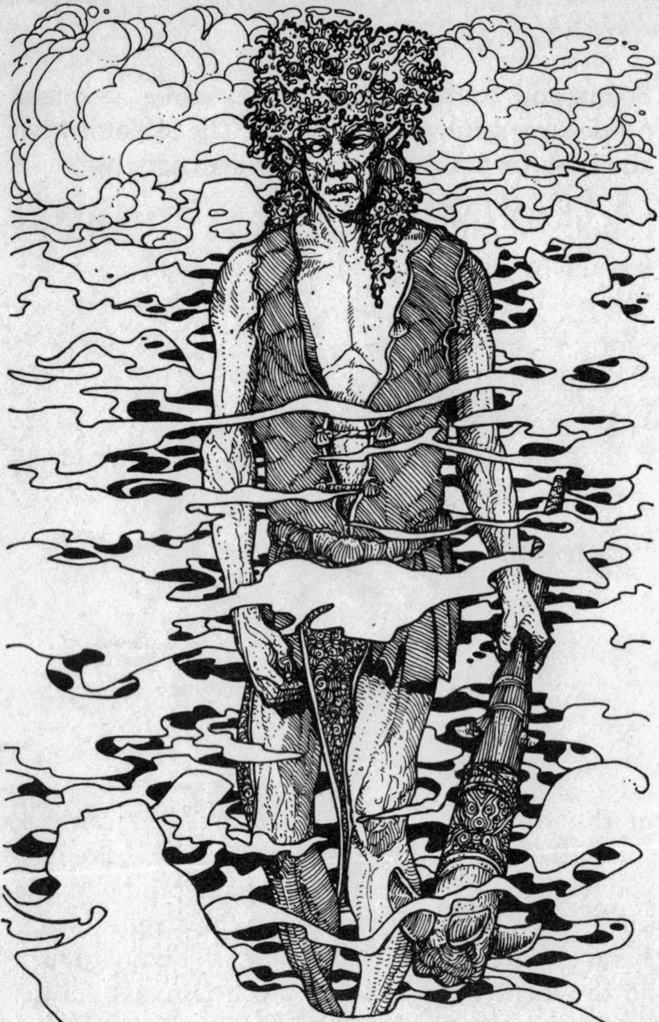

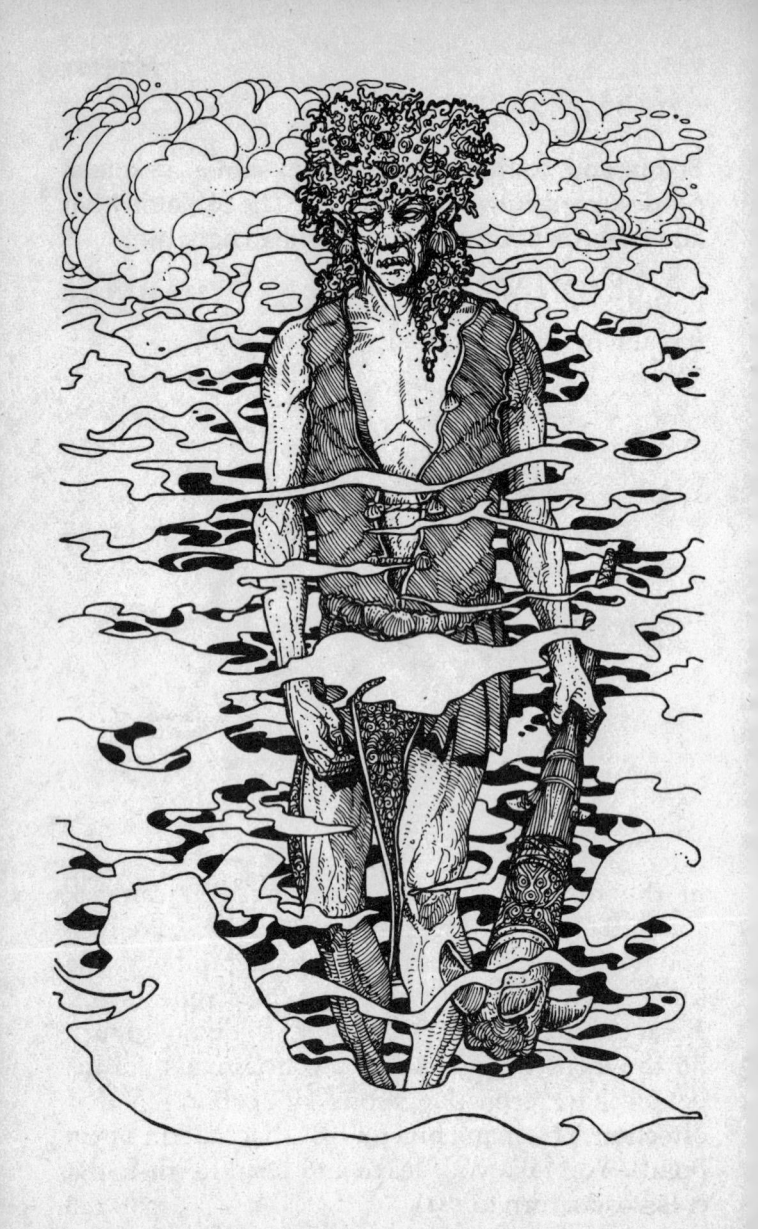

## 102

You beach your boat and look around. To the west is a trail leading towards the hilly interior of the island, and to the south there is a tall white cliff which bars your way. Appearing out of the wispy mist to the north looms a huge figure – a giant, almost sixteen feet tall, clad in green and his hair a tangle of kelp and shells that he wears for decoration. He is muscular and carries a massive club. 'Hello, human,' he booms. Will you:

| | |
|---|---|
| Attack him? | Turn to 240 |
| Greet him in return? | Turn to 328 |
| Run away to the west? | Turn to 257 |

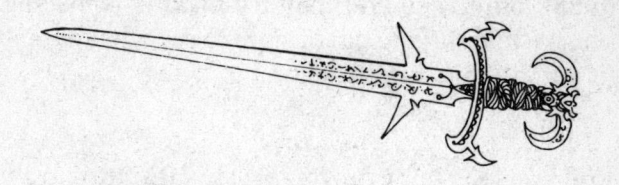

## 103

You set off on a fine day, with the cries of seabirds in your ears, and before long you arrive at a crossroads. By the side of the path to the north, there stands a wooden pole with a skull atop it. By the southern path, there is a bloodied fistful of bird's feathers on a pointed stick. There is nothing to mark the path which continues westwards. Will you:

| | |
|---|---|
| Go north? | Turn to 327 |
| Go west? | Turn to 181 |
| Go south? | Turn to 128 |

## 104

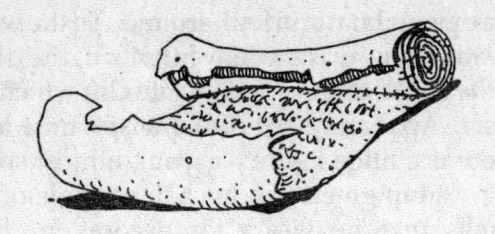

After a few minutes, you hear the sound of footsteps coming down the passage from beyond the railinged gates. Taking a careful peek, you observe a Goblin who is standing idly by them on the other side! You can either keep still and do nothing (turn to 88); otherwise you may try making some slight noise while staying out of sight to see what happens (if you do this, turn to 348).

## 105

Will you take out a pewter ale tankard (turn to 276), a pair of bone dice (turn to 41), or both items if you have both (turn to 276)?

## 106

Now the passageway branches. You can continue on eastwards or you can take a side-turning to the north. Daylight gleams faintly from the northern passage, but you can also hear faint rending sounds that are not at all pleasant coming from that direction. If you wish to go east, turn to **253**. If you wish to go north, turn to **155**.

## 107

You open the door quietly and discover a comfortably appointed room lit with ornate wall-lamps. There are fine carpets, a large cushion, and wall-paintings decorating the room; lying on a fur-covered bed a man wearing a chain-mail vest is sleeping. A sword is scabbarded at his belt. Will you:

| | |
|---|---|
| Leave him and open the southern door? | Turn to **245** |
| Kill him? | Turn to **290** |
| Wake him and try to talk with him? | Turn to **43** |

## 108

The old man looks pitiful and defeated as he sees a fresh tormentor advancing on him – or so he thinks. Gently, you help him up. Do you have a bunch of keys? If you do, turn to **289**. If you don't, turn to **369**.

## 109

The snakes lunge forward to attack, and one bites through your leather leggings; the venomous fangs sink into your flesh. Other bites follow, and you fall, dying from the effects of the deadly poison. You have failed in your quest.

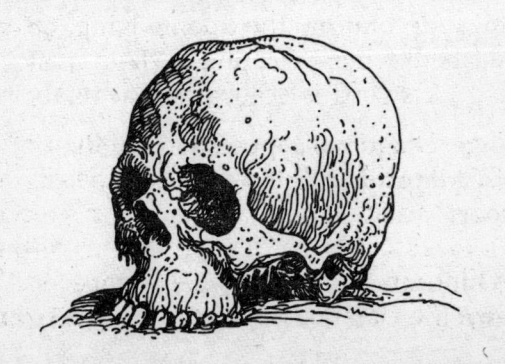

## 110

You have made it to the balcony much faster than the wizard expected, for your 'Speed' spell countered the Spell of 'Slowing' he placed on the steps.

Mordraneth reaches for his sword, but you are very fast and you strike him, causing 2 points of damage. Turn to **46** to finish the fight, and deduct 2 points from Mordraneth's STAMINA score as given in that paragraph!

## 111

The huge Dragon disappears – another of Mordraneth's illusions! By now, you're hardly aware what is real and what is not – but such a spectacular illusion must surely be close to the lair of the evil wizard himself . . . you cross the chamber and press on, down the violet passage beyond. Turn to **150**.

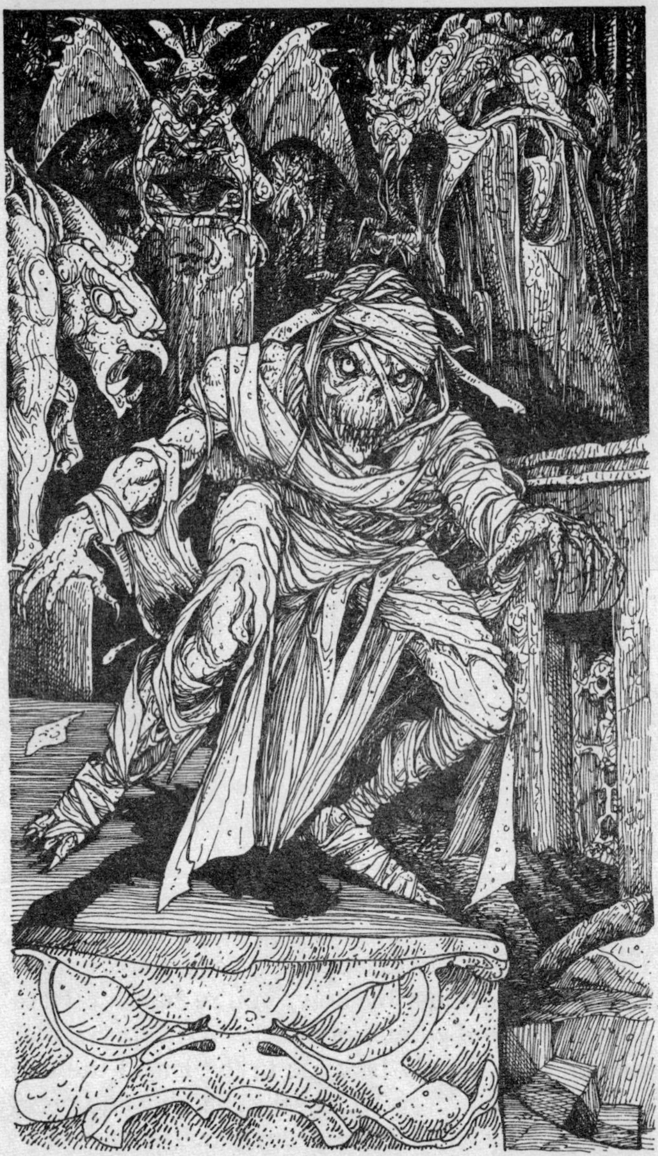

## 112

You move along the grey passageway, and the air strikes chilly and dank. Horribly, behind you the passageway starts to shrink away to nothing, closing up behind you, and you have to run to avoid being swallowed up by it. You run into a chamber which is the colour of yellowed, leprous bone, and you see tombs and great sepulchres stretching out before you. Steps lead down to crypts with barred doors of bronze and brass. The place is bone-numbingly cold, and a low moaning starts to fill the air. Suddenly, before your horrified eyes, a spectral shrouded figure rises up from the cold stone and lunges at you with icy taloned claw-like hands. You will have to fight for your life! This is not an illusion!

SPECTRE          SKILL 7          STAMINA 7

Each time the Spectre hits you, you must deduct 1 SKILL point; this loss is *permanent* until you find some magical way of remedying the loss. If you win, turn to **189**.

## 113

You feel that you could perhaps knock down the door, but this would require some hefty kicking and you might lose some of your STAMINA. You could also alert guards or monsters around the place. Do you want to try battering down the door (turn to **294**), or do you want to return to the main passage and open the door at the end of it (turn to **124**)?

## 114

You stand before a door marked with a black and amber cross. You decide to open it, to see what lies on the other side. Turn to **393**.

## 115

The illusion just disappears at the very moment when you 'kill' it, and you realize what it was. But it was no mere illusion, for it had enough reality about it to harm you! The magic in this place is growing more dangerous . . . You step through the gap at the end of the passage. Turn to **203**.

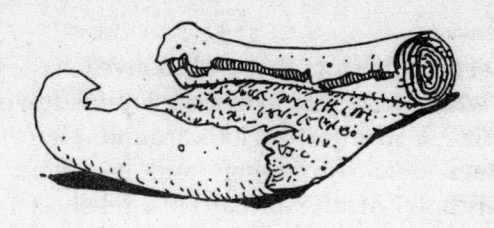

## 116

You run a good distance westwards to get away from the skeletal figure, but it does not seem to be pursuing you. You breathe a sigh of relief. Turn to **356**.

## 117

Breathing heavily, you push away the body of the evil cleric with your foot; as you do so, a pouch he had at his belt spills out 5 Gold Pieces (add these to your Treasure on your *Adventure Sheet*). As you look around, it dawns upon you how evil this place is; you sense an emanation of evil from the altar, and there are dread wall-paintings showing scenes of unspeakable horror. One in particular captures your attention: a black skull with livid red eyes, floating in the air above a rocky crevasse, gloating over the terrified ghostly forms of spirits of the dead. But there's no shelter to be found outside, so you will have to sleep here. You look around and discover a trapdoor beneath a carpet in front of the altar; you pull the Dark Priest's body over it to stop anything getting in, then settle down to sleep. Now you must *Test your Luck*. If you are Lucky, turn to **237**. If you are Unlucky, turn to **279**.

## 118

You set off north together and soon reach the giant's cave, which is set into a hillside sloping down to the shoreline. You enter and look around. There's some fine fish stew simmering, and he offers you a HUGE bowl of it! You eat with relish. The giant looks thoughtful and says, 'This is becoming an increasingly evil place. I'm not afraid, for I can look after myself, but you . . . you must be on some kind of quest here.' You nod, but say nothing, determined to give nothing away. 'I don't know if this will help you, but it might mean something,' he says, and he retrieves an old scroll which he had carefully hidden under a large pile of shells and conches. You read it:

> Singing in the wind is the harbinger of death, and the Stealer of Souls shall tear terrors from the minds of the damned to make his home.

It seems to make little sense to you, nor can you make out all of the date inscribed in one corner. The numbers are smudged, and only three are legible: 3 . . . 5 . . . 0 in that order. But you thank the giant; he tells you you can keep the scroll (add the Message Scroll to the list of Equipment Carried on your *Adventure Sheet* and make a note of the date numbers – 350 – too). Soon it begins to rain heavily and you stay in the giant's cave for the night.

The next morning is sunny and clear; the giant wishes you well and gives you some salted fish, enough for three meals (add 3 to your Provisions).

You set off to the west, to seek the trail leading inland; turn to **257**.

### 119

'You wretched coward, how do you expect to gain glory and respect?', hisses the lizard contemptuously. It pronounces a curse upon you and then disappears. You must lose 1 LUCK point, and flee south in fear! Turn to **54**.

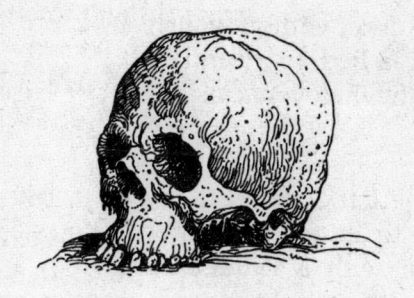

### 120

A dirty, cluttered room, crudely furnished and with doors leading in several directions, greets your eyes, but you have no time to take in all the details! There are two Goblins here, and they leap up to attack you. In the doorway, you can fight them one at a time.

|               | SKILL | STAMINA |
|---------------|-------|---------|
| First GOBLIN  | 5     | 5       |
| Second GOBLIN | 5     | 6       |

If you win, turn to **300**.

## 121

Beyond the door, a torch-lit corridor extends southwards. You move softly along it, until you come to a door at the end. Even from a few yards away, you can hear guttural talk and raucous laughter from within, but you don't recognize the language. Will you:

| | |
|---|---|
| Head back north? | Turn to 376 |
| Open the door, sword in hand, to fight? | Turn to 25 |
| Open the door, without your sword readied, to try and talk with whatever is inside? | Turn to 209 |

## 122

You take the dark tunnel to the west, using your light source to illuminate your way. You step into a high cavern with a vaulted roof; from a ceiling encrusted with stalactites water drips, nourishing thick growths of grey and white fungi which cluster on the floor. You can just make out a passage exiting to the west of where you stand. Do you want to continue on westwards (turn to 51) or try eating one or two of the fungi (turn to 345)?

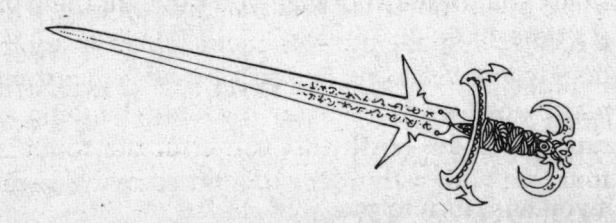

## 123

The small room beyond is plainly furnished with chairs and a small table on which you see a decanter of white wine, some cheeses, and a fruit pie. You suddenly feel hungry! If you wish, you may eat a meal from what is on the table (regaining 2 STAMINA points), and you can take the cheese for another meal later (add 1 to your Provisions on your *Adventure Sheet*). There is a small door in the south wall of this room, and you decide to open this after checking for noise and hearing nothing. Turn to **50**.

## 124

You open the door and walk into a large chamber constructed of bare stone with high walls, lit by torches which burn and spit, giving off blue light and faintly greenish smoke. This smoke is unpleasant, irritating your throat and nostrils. There is a half-open door in the east wall, from behind which a red glow spills into this room. There is another door in the west wall, and this is made of very stout black wood with massively thick iron banding and fittings. In the north-east corner of the room is a fountain with a thin jet of liquid spraying several feet into the air. Will you:

| Drink some water from the fountain? | Turn to **306** |
|---|---|
| Toss a Gold Piece into the fountain and make a wish? | Turn to **177** |
| Open the west door? | Turn to **373** |
| Cross to the east door and look round it? | Turn to **28** |

### 125

Passing along the rainbow passage, you feel an unfamiliar sense of goodness. Another illusion, perhaps? The passage leads into a high-ceilinged chamber filled with rainbow-coloured lights. Inside, there are three semi-transparent human figures, and also three passages which exit on the far side of the chamber: one yellow-green, one azure, and one a deep ochre colour. One of the shimmering figures drifts soundlessly towards you. 'Brave friend, not everything here has been corrupted by the wicked one. He has not overcome all of us. Let me give you a blessing to aid you,' and he stretches out his hands to touch your head. Will you:

| Let the figure touch you? | Turn to **398** |
|---|---|
| Run to the yellow-green passage? | Turn to **307** |
| Run to the azure passage? | Turn to **272** |
| Run to the ochre passage? | Turn to **77** |

## 126

Your magical Ring of Fire Resistance minimizes the damage you take; lose only 1 STAMINA point. But now you are close to the balcony, and you will be able to fight the wizard on equal terms as you move in! Turn to **46**.

## 127

You are in combat with a Giant Stormbird; you must fight it alone, since the sailors are too far away and can't get to aid you through the rain and gale and lashing waves which spill on to the deck.

GIANT STORMBIRD     SKILL 8     STAMINA 12

If you are slain by the Stormbird's slashing talons and cruel beak, your first adventure has ended here! If you win, turn to **167**.

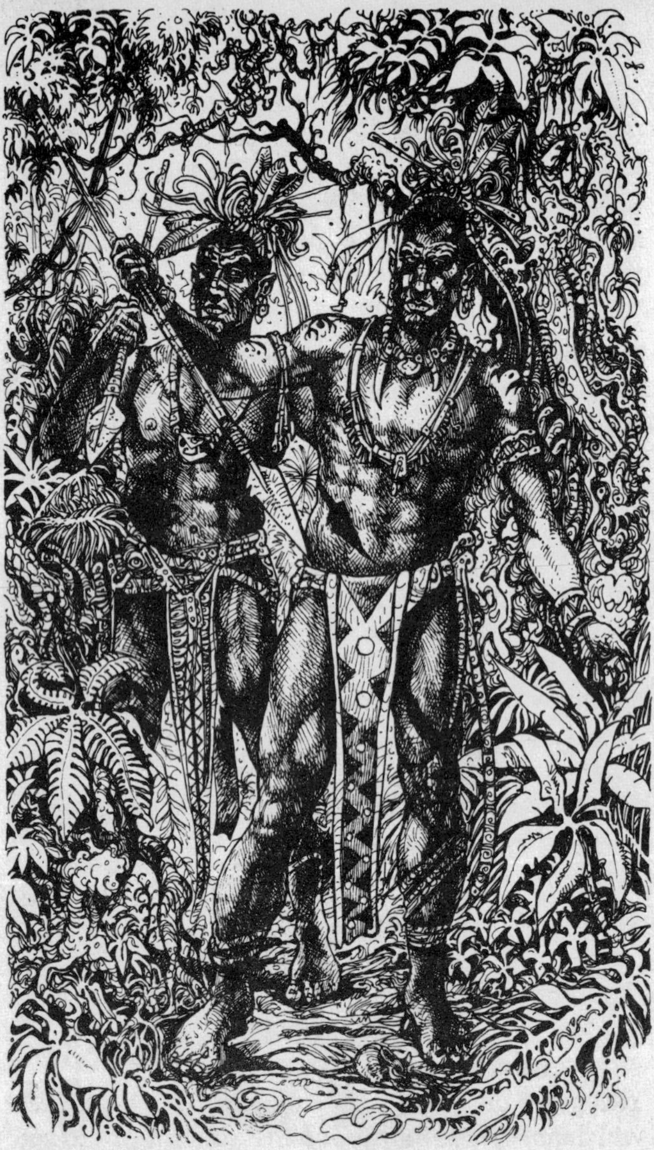

## 128

The trail grows more overgrown as it descends into thick, verdant vegetation: masses of bushes, ferns, vines and trailing roots . . . gaudy insects buzz lazily around in the air. It is very warm and humid, and you use up a lot of energy hacking your way through the undergrowth in overgrown parts of the trail. Deduct 2 points from your STAMINA.

Suddenly two men just seem to melt out of the bushes beside the trail and stand before you! They are dark-skinned and wear loincloths, and they carry spears. These they point towards you and gesture wildly – you have no idea what it is they're trying to tell you, but their spears are sharp! Will you:

| | |
|---|---|
| Attack them? | Turn to 310 |
| Try to greet them in some way? | Turn to 168 |
| Offer them a Gold Piece? | Turn to 224 |

## 129

You press on south, ignoring a turning to the east which only leads to the Goblins' room. Turn to 268.

## 130

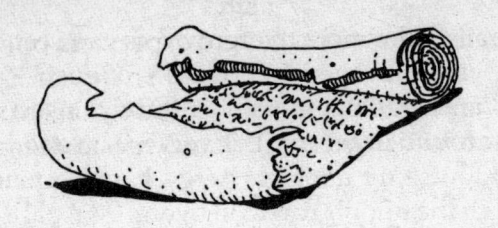

The Troll has 2 Gold Pieces in a pouch, and under the pillow of his bed you find another 2 Gold Pieces (add these to your Treasure on your *Adventure Sheet*). On the table, among a jumble of cutlery and earthenware plates, jugs and bottles of brown liquid (which you wisely ignore), you find a bunch of keys. If you wish to take these, add them to the list of Equipment Carried on your *Adventure Sheet*.

By the time you have finished your search, acrid smoke is beginning to drift under the door in the west wall and a small cloud is beginning to coalesce. Escape to the west is obviously impossible, and you have to get out before you are suffocated by the thick smoke, so you must try the eastern door; turn to **260**.

## 131

Peering through the grille, you can just make out two slumped human bodies lying on a pile of filthy straw inside a dank, unlit cell. Will you try to open the door and help these people (turn to **18**) or turn back and go south (turn to **227**)?

## 132

You search through a litter of papers and bric-à-brac which fills the guard's room. There seems to be nothing valuable, but you do find a sheet of vellum covered with ornate, bold handwriting. It reads:

> I need to know by the end of today how the meddling wizard learnt to use magic I did not teach him, here in the Crypts. If he will not talk before the end of day, have the torturer put him to death by fire. Mehrabian will assist, and of course those dark, pointy-eared little fellows will want to watch. I have better things to do with my time.

It is signed, simply, 'M'.

Puzzling over this, you leave through the west door of the dining room. Turn to **17**.

## 133

The 'Restore Skill' spell allows you to recover lost SKILL points. You may cast this spell at any time except during combats, and you will be able to recover up to 3 lost SKILL points. Return to **188**.

## 134

Your goodly thought is reflected back upon you; as you utter words of blessing, the air seems almost to thaw slightly, and you hear what sounds like a collective sigh from the souls of the dead which hover here. Regain 1 SKILL point and 1 LUCK point. Now, you can either take the airy, light exit-passage (turn to 319) or the dark-brown, earthy way out (turn to 247).

### 135

You head for the cottage, approach the open doorway and peer in. The windows are shuttered and little light penetrates inside – but in the room you can see someone tied to a chair; he tries to raise a hand but cannot sustain the effort, and groans heavily. He is clearly weak and in pain. Will you:

| | |
|---|---|
| Look more closely round the room? | Turn to 215 |
| Go in and untie the man? | Turn to 183 |
| Ignore him and head back south? | Turn to 250 |

### 136

You head north along the passage until you come to an eastward passage. Opposite this is a faintly carved wall-carving of some kind. Will you:

| | |
|---|---|
| Look closely at the wall-carving? | Turn to 216 |
| Follow the passage north? | Turn to 184 |
| Take the passage east? | Turn to 72 |
| Retrace your steps back south? | Turn to 129 |

### 137

You collect 6 Gold Pieces from the Orcs (add this to your Treasure on your *Adventure Sheet*); if you gambled with them and lost, you can take back the money you lost (and the bone dice as well if you lost those too!). The dice the Orcs had are shoddy, and their ale and rat-pasties are revolting. You can now either go back to the north (turn to **346**) or open the east door (turn to **4**).

## 138

You apply the oil to the lock and hinges, so long rusted. Cross the oil off the list of Equipment Carried on your *Adventure Sheet*. By a little tinkering with the lock you get something to click, and you can now open the door and look inside. The room is very small and dark, and is lined with shelves, almost all of which are empty. However, in a small wooden box on one shelf, you find three blocks of incense which smell sweet and fragrant even though they must have been here for years. You take these, so add them to the list of Equipment Carried on your *Adventure Sheet*. You go back to the main passageway, and now you can try opening the western door (turn to **358**) or you can press on southwards (turn to **283**).

## 139

It occurs to you that the man's chain-mail armour was surely superior to your own leather armour; sadly, however, your final blow ripped away one side of it so that it is now useless. Cursing your misfortune, you leave the room and open the southern door in the next room; turn to **245**.

## 140

You look for the man's clothes and find a set of ornately decorated wizard's robes on a peg in this room. You hand them to the old man, who gratefully exchanges them for the rags he was kept in.

'Thank you,' says the wizard. 'My name is Alsander.' As you had hoped, the wizard you were sent to rescue! Excitedly, you tell him who sent you, and your purpose here. Alsander listens intently, but then shakes his head sadly. 'Ah, cunning Mordraneth. Of course; he fooled Vanestin into a wild goose chase in Allansia. Now Vanestin and the other wizards won't be able to resist him when he lands in Pollua.' You look at Alsander, puzzled;

what can he mean? The wizard soon enlightens you.

'Mordraneth isn't in Allansia at all. He's here. He is scheming a monstrous evil, deep within the foundation of the Iron Crypts, in his Empire of Illusions, as he calls it. There he is harnessing a dreadful power, one to drive men to madness and death, in order to unleash it on Pollua to bring him still greater power. If he can achieve his goal, none could challenge him.'

This is dire news indeed . . . but an idea is beginning to form at the back of your mind. When first you were asked to rescue Alsander, you regretted losing the opportunity for glory which ridding the world of Mordraneth would bring. You ask Alsander to continue. Turn to **325**.

## 141

You wedge the crowbar between the walls and run. The stout metal holds the walls apart for only a few seconds before it buckles and snaps, but it's just long enough. You make it to the dark tunnel as the walls clash together a few feet behind you. Turn to **296**.

## 142

You leap and bound up the stairs at twice normal speed, totally confounding the wizard who was trying to prepare another spell. Now he reaches for his sword; while he does, you can strike at him, causing him the loss of 2 STAMINA points. Turn to **46** to continue the fight, and don't forget to subtract 2 points from Mordraneth's STAMINA score given there!

## 143

One of the sailors gives you a small jar of ointment (add this to the list of Equipment Carried on your *Adventure Sheet*). He explains that on the Isle of Despair there may be insects which bite and spread disease, and this will help repel them. He commends you on your bravery and says he hopes his gift will help you. You thank him, and collect your gear for the adventure to come. Turn to **249**.

## 144

The shaman looks disappointed, and soon after you are taken to a small, dirty hut where you will sleep. However, you are disturbed by a lizard which scuttles about on the earth floor all night and keeps waking you up; moreover, you can't find it to kill it! Lack of sleep means that you must lose 2 STAMINA points. Turn to **101**.

## 145

You can just make out the shape of a slim body which is limed over and encrusted with stalagmites. It will take you a couple of hours to chip away the chalky deposit and find out what lies beneath. If you wish to do this, turn to **266**. If you decide not to bother, but to press onwards, turn to **156**.

## 146

You search desperately for a way out and at last, behind the wall-hanging, you find a concealed door! You tug it open, and gulp down the cleaner air outside. As you are about to step through, you hear a small voice calling in the air to your left, 'Hey! Don't leave me here! I can be of help.' The smoke swirls around your feet . . . will you go on through the door and up the stairs beyond, shutting the door behind you (turn to **58**), or will you check carefully in that part of the room where you heard the voice (turn to **334**)?

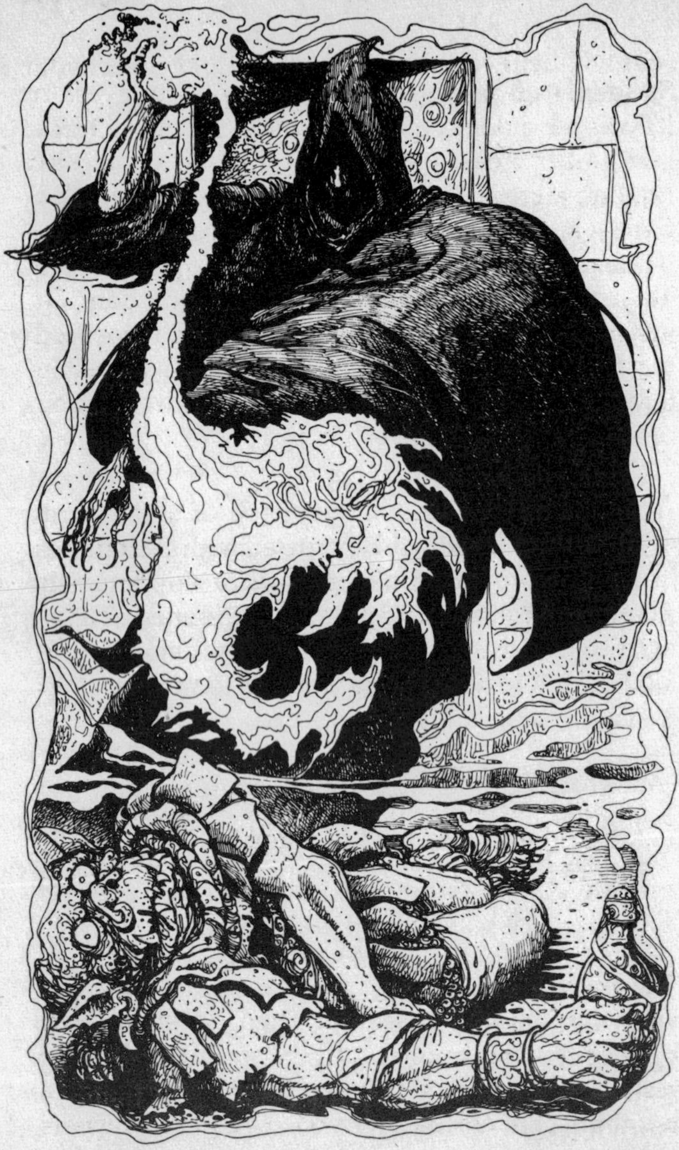

## 147

Suddenly a brief vision passes before your eyes! In it, you see a door before you, marked with a black and amber cross, and beyond the door is an Orc holding a brass flask. You move forward and slay him – but then into the room steps a fearsome black-robed figure who unleashes a spell at you! Then the vision is gone. Was it a premonition? Or just an illusion? You make a note to be well prepared for combat should you come across such a door! You leave the Orcs' bedroom, enter the guardroom, and open the south door. Turn to **333**.

## 148

You wade in, fighting on the side of one Orc against the other, who is soon killed. You take no damage in the battle. 'Fanks,' says the Orc you helped. 'I allus 'ated 'im – nah I can git me money back worrie stole offa me.' The Orc bends down to take a leather pouch from the body. Will you:

| | |
|---|---:|
| Leave this room and head west along the passage? | Turn to **97** |
| Attack the single Orc remaining? | Turn to **380** |
| Talk to the Orc? | Turn to **33** |

## 149

The passageway is very dark, and you must use your light source to see by. Then, suddenly, the light source winks out and you can do nothing to restore it! You are enveloped in darkness, and a numbing chill creeps over you. You hear whispers around you, and scuttlings and squeaks; then you hear a ghastly sound: the scraping of iron-hard claws on stone – or is it the sound of a meat cleaver being sharpened? It is getting closer, and a guttural chuckling accompanies it. You can feel the fear creeping into your bones, and you shiver. Darkness deeper than any night is sinking into your very marrow. Will you:

| | |
|---|---|
| Cast a 'Dispel Illusion' spell, if you can? | Turn to 391 |
| Cast a 'Dispel Fear' spell, if you can? | Turn to 200 |
| Flee into the darkness, although you do not know where you are going? | Turn to 382 |

### 150

The violet passage soon opens into a large, cratered cavern, littered with rocks and cobwebs; you think you see a single exit in the distance, but it is obscured by a huge rock, several yards across. Then the rock moves – it is no rock at all! Yellow-black, hairy legs seem to spring out in all directions, and a bony black head rears up, showing razor-sharp mandibles. The wings on this mammoth Spider's back buzz and flutter, but it moves towards you on its great, springing legs. You sense that this is an illusion, but one of exceptional strength. Waves of fear radiate from the thing; you must deduct 1 point from your SKILL *temporarily* (during this combat) and lose 2 points of STAMINA due to this fear. If you can, you have time to cast a 'Dispel Fear' spell, which negates these effects. As the Spider closes in, will you use a 'Dispel Illusion' spell (turn to 371) or fight the monster with your sword (turn to 175)?

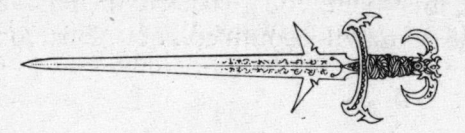

## 151

You drag the entangling strands away from your throat and struggle on, but you have to lose 3 STAMINA points because of the effects of strangulation. Now, at last, you're on the balcony and you can fight the wizard with your sword. Turn to 46.

## 152

The passageway at the end of the sewer forks. You may follow either the yellow-green one (turn to 307) or one which is filled with rainbow-coloured light (turn to 125).

## 153

Inside the chest you find a small casket of fragrant sandalwood, inlaid with fine mother-of-pearl. This contains two items, wrapped in silk. One is a bronze ring; you do not know what this does. The other is a tiny platinum amulet with ornate marks etched very finely on it, on a silver filigree chain. You know intuitively that this has some magical power, but you can't tell what this might be. You can carry, or wear, either or both of these items; if you do, add the Bronze Ring and/or the Platinum Amulet to the list of Equipment Carried on your *Adventure Sheet*. Leaving this room, you go back to the passage, and open the door at the south end of it. Turn to **124**.

### 154

Before long, the passageway divides; to the north is a low tunnel which clearly opens into a daylit chamber, from which a high-pitched squeaking sound, interspersed with a deeper noise almost like a growl, resounds down the tunnel. If you want to investigate the chamber at the end of that tunnel, turn to **385**. Or you can continue westwards; turn to **274**.

### 155

The daylight grows clearer as you make your way up the passageway towards the tunnel. Now you hear the noise more clearly, it sounds as if something or someone is being ripped limb from limb by some snarling monster. Undeterred, you decide to move in and find out just what's in there! Turn to **385**.

## 156

You trudge south along the passageway which seems to wind on interminably. Finally, you come to a T-junction, and from here you can head either east (turn to **285**) or west (turn to **356**).

## 157

Using your lantern, you descend the steeply cut stone steps to the winding limestone passages below. These twist and turn, and you seem to spend hours travelling with only faint sounds of dripping water for company. You must stop to eat a meal during your travels or deduct 2 points from your STAMINA. Next, you must *Test your Luck*. If you are Lucky, turn to **388**. If you are Unlucky, turn to **85**.

## 158

You must now *Test your Luck*. If you are Lucky, turn to **239**. If you are Unlucky, turn to **338**.

## 159

All you find for your trouble is a large centipede that scuttles out from under a rock and nips you with its poisonous bite. You crush it angrily under your heel, but you suffer the loss of 2 STAMINA points. Turn to 337.

## 160

The light in the passageway seems to grow a little brighter as you make your way along, and you observe that ahead it turns north. Peering round the bend, you see that the passage opens into a lit chamber. Inside the chamber is a table bearing gold which gleams in the light of an oil lamp fixed to the wall above, and there is a door in the west wall of the chamber. However, you can also hear someone – or something – lumbering about in there, out of sight. If you want to enter the chamber, turn to 225. If you would rather turn back down the passage and then set off towards the west, turn to 255.

## 161

Unfortunately, although the Orcs seem friendly at first, one of them is a bit less drunk than the others and it eyes you over as you sit sipping the foul ale they have given you. 'I ain't seen 'im befur,' it growls as it gobbles down a rat-pasty. 'I don't fink 'e's wiv our lot.' The other Orcs suddenly look nasty, and reach for their weapons. You must fight them, so turn to 185.

## 162

You swing the grappling iron up to the ledge and shin up the rope. The wind clutches at your clothes as you crouch, exposed to the elements outside. You try not to look at what the Razorbeak Bird was eating, and you check through the nest. You find a headband of black cotton, with a motif executed in silver thread on it; this depicts a spider with a staff superimposed diagonally across it. You may take this and wear it if you wish; if you do, add the Spider Headband to the list of Equipment Carried on your *Adventure Sheet*. You clamber back down and set off southwards; turn to **42**.

## 163

While the warrior's sword is inferior to your own, his chain-mail armour is definitely superior. (Add this to the list of Equipment Carried on your *Adventure Sheet*.) When you wear it, it will increase your SKILL score permanently by 1 point; this *does* allow you to exceed your *Initial* SKILL score, *unless* that was originally 11 or 12.

Pleased with your superior armour, and flushed with the success of the combat, you leave this room and open the south door in the adjoining room; turn to **245**.

## 164

As you attempt to open the chest, a scything blade swings up from a crack in the stone floor and cuts deeply into your flesh. So severe is the wound that you must lose 1 point from your SKILL and 6 points from your STAMINA. If the injury is not enough to kill you, you give a scream of agony and pass out from pain and shock. When you come round, you can try again to open the chest (turn to **246**) or go back to the main passage and open the door at the southern end of it (turn to **124**).

## 165

You take just a sip of the liquid – and spit out rancid vinegar. A loud laugh echoes down the corridor. 'Oh, you poor fool! Don't you recognize an Archmage when you meet one? I'm going to have fun watching your slow death. I couldn't let you die that easily!' and the voice subsides into mocking laughter. You can see no-one but you know this is Mordraneth. You are filled with hatred for your tormentor, and you get up and struggle onwards; turn to **387**.

## 166

The Fire Globe surrounds you in burning flame and suffocating smoke! Suffer the loss of 6 STAMINA points. If you are still alive, you race onwards, and make it to the balcony where Mordraneth stands. Turn to **110**.

## 167

Did you turn your back and try to flee before fighting the Stormbird? If you did, turn to **347**. If you made no attempt to run away, turn to **223**.

## 168

You advance with palms outstretched. The men realize you aren't hostile, so they lower their spears – a little! They guide you along the path and after an hour or so they usher you into their village. Turn to **208**.

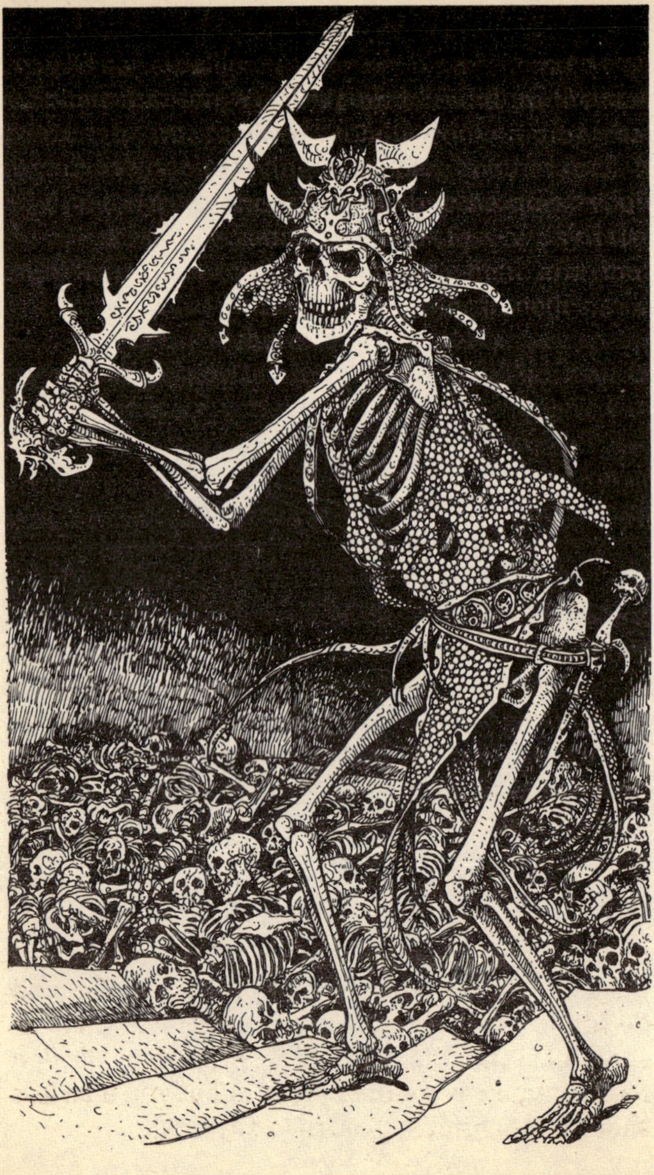

## 169

You are fighting a Skeletal Warrior, who swings at you with great strength; his massive two-handed sword glints as it sweeps through the air in an arc towards you. May the gods grant you good luck in this dangerous combat!

SKELETAL WARRIOR  SKILL 10  STAMINA 10

If you win, turn to **236**.

## 170

As the beetle-thing lunges at you, your medallion shines with pure white light, a beam of which hits the illusion, dispersing it into nothingness. You see the gap in the wall at the end of the passage, and decide to make for it. You are unnerved, and the shock of seeing the gruesomely convincing illusion has cost you 1 point of STAMINA, but you'll be less shockable in future . . . turn to **203**.

## 171

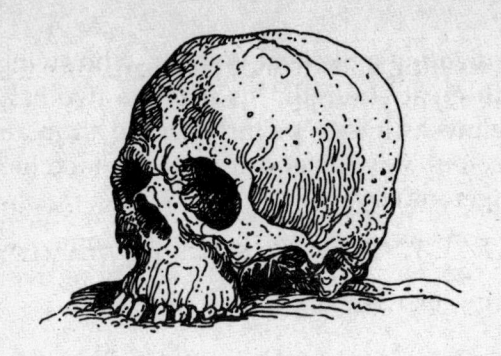

You cannot open this door by any means available to you. Frustrated, you set off in an easterly direction. Turn to **114**.

## 172

You try to open the eastern door, but it is locked. Do you have an Ebony Key? If you do, turn to **201**. If you don't, turn to **113**.

## 173

The snakes lunge forward to attack, and you feel a pair of fangs sink through your leather leggings into your flesh, then another bite . . . you hack at the reptiles with your sword, but it is useless, there are so many of them. You collapse from the venom, and death is near. You have failed in your quest.

## 174

Are you wearing a bronze ring? If you are, turn to **297**. If you are not, turn to **30**.

## 175
Are you wearing a headband? If you are, turn to **198**. If you aren't, turn to **394**.

## 176
The 'Luck' spell allows you to recover lost LUCK points. You can cast this spell at any time except during a combat, and you will be able to recover up to 3 lost LUCK points. Return to **188**.

## 177
As you think about making your wish, you notice that bubbles are forming on the surface of the Gold Piece. The liquid isn't water, it is acid! You move away from the fountain, and now you can either open the west door (turn to **373**) or look round the east door (turn to **28**).

## 178
As you prise the brick away, you reveal a small cavity behind it within which is a small, black, wooden box with clasps of brass. Will you:

| Open the box? | Turn to 374 |
| Go back to the southern passage and open the door at the end of it? | Turn to 227 |
| Go back to the southern passage and look for the secret door the man mentioned? | Turn to 98 |

## 179

You leap aside just as a spear hurtles past you, triggered by a trap linked to the door. The spear impales itself in the door opposite you; moments later, you hear sounds to the north, so you decide to set off southwards! Turn to 283.

## 180

'Vat's not very friendly,' growls a half-drunk Orc. His companions agree, but they are enjoying their beer and seem unsure whether to be aggressive or to get on with their drinking. Roll one die; on a roll of 1–3, the Orcs do get nasty and you will have to fight them, so turn to 185. On a roll of 4–6, the Orcs carry on drinking and accept your company after all; turn to 254.

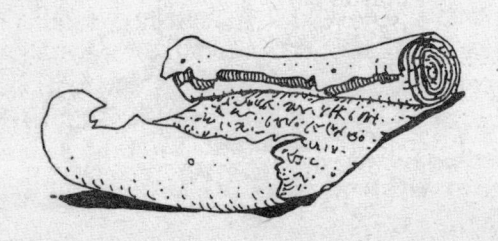

## 181

Having reached the crossroads on the trail, you set off west along the unmarked path. You are heading into undulating low foothills, and your legs grow tired as you march. There are craggy peaks to the north, and the trail turns north-west towards them. It is late afternoon when you begin to grow hungry, and you must stop and eat a meal. The rays of the setting sun bathe the countryside in a warm glow and reflect back from some kind of small building, made of grey rock, to the west. You could reach it in an hour. You can either make for the building (turn to 379) or continue on the trail (turn to 53).

## 182

You soon find the giant's cave which is set into a hillside. A quick but careful check reveals that no other creature is here, but you can smell fish stew! You enter. There is enough fish stew for two meals (you can eat one or both of them here, but you cannot carry stew with you). After you have eaten, rested and recovered STAMINA points, do you want to return westwards to the trail (turn to 257) or search the cave (turn to 301)?

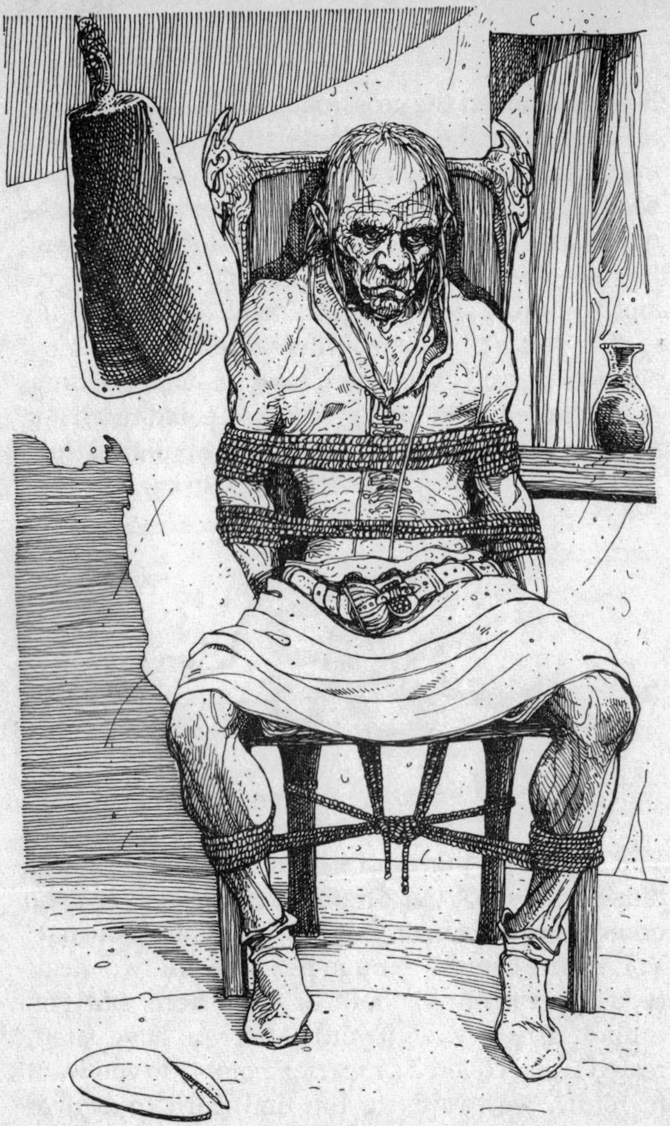

## 183

You stride in – triggering a tripwire trap: a weight strung from the ceiling falls and hits you hard across the shoulders; deduct 4 STAMINA points. 'Tried . . . to warn . . .' gasps the man, and slumps back in the chair. Groaning from the pain of bruised muscles, you untie him; turn to 71.

## 184

The passageway ends at a door facing you. Even from outside, you can detect a rather unpleasant, foetid smell. You hear a faint scratching and scrabbling coming from behind the door. You can either open the door and see what lies beyond it (turn to 6) or retrace your steps back south (turn to 303).

## 185

In this room, you must fight the Orcs two at a time until you have killed two and only one remains for you to finish off. Roll two dice for yourself and for *both* your opponents; add relevant SKILL scores; the combatant with the highest Attack Strength is the one who will land an effective blow during that Attack Round. Fortunately, the Orcs are somewhat drunk, so their SKILL scores are lower than usual.

|            | SKILL | STAMINA |
|------------|-------|---------|
| First ORC  | 4     | 5       |
| Second ORC | 4     | 4       |
| Third ORC  | 4     | 5       |

If you win, turn to 73.

## 186

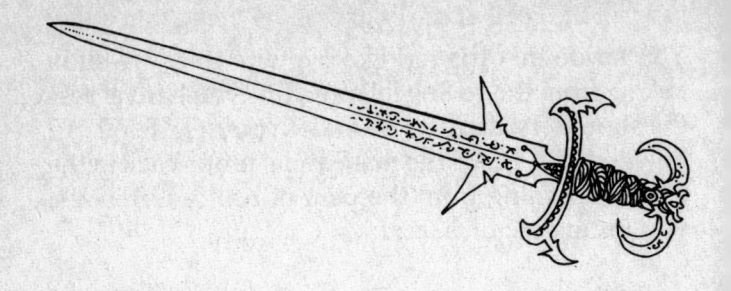

The Birdman flies away before you can reach him. Outside, however, you see him glide down and make cawing calls and whoops; and other Birdmen are gathering, joining him . . . you'd better not hang around! Turn to **292**.

## 187

Such a hard fight, and an adversary who used magic against you! Could it be . . . ? Surely not. Although you were told that only Mordraneth's own spells would work in the Iron Crypts, this must have been a minion instructed by Mordraneth. And your job is to find Alsander in any event . . . Will you:

| | |
|---|---|
| Search the bodies? | Turn to **353** |
| Try the east door in the Orc's room? | Turn to **123** |
| Look through the south door the Dark Priest entered by? | Turn to **82** |

## 188

You may choose *three* spells only from the list below. To help you make a wise choice, you may wish to read all the spell descriptions. After being told about a spell, you will be sent back to this paragraph. When you have decided which three spells to learn, make a note of them, and the effects they have and when they can be used. Unless otherwise stated, each spell may be used only once. Then, turn to **61**.

The spells you may choose from are:

| | |
|---|---|
| 'Dispel Fear' | Turn to 2 |
| 'Dispel Illusion' | Turn to 295 |
| 'Fire Globe' | Turn to 16 |
| 'Healing' | Turn to 336 |
| 'Luck' spell | Turn to 176 |
| 'Restore Skill' | Turn to 133 |
| 'Speed' | Turn to 213 |

## 189

Fearing further horrors like the Spectre, you look around in desperation. At the end of the huge hall of cold stone tombs you can make out three passageways and you must follow one. Will you take:

| | |
|---|---|
| The green passage? | Turn to 395 |
| The rainbow-coloured passage? | Turn to 125 |
| The yellow-green passage? | Turn to 307 |

## 190

Mordraneth laughs as the Fire Globe smashes into you, causing you the loss of 6 STAMINA points. If you are still alive, you keep on up the stairs to challenge his foul sorcery with your trusty sword, and you reach the balcony on which he stands! Turn to **46**.

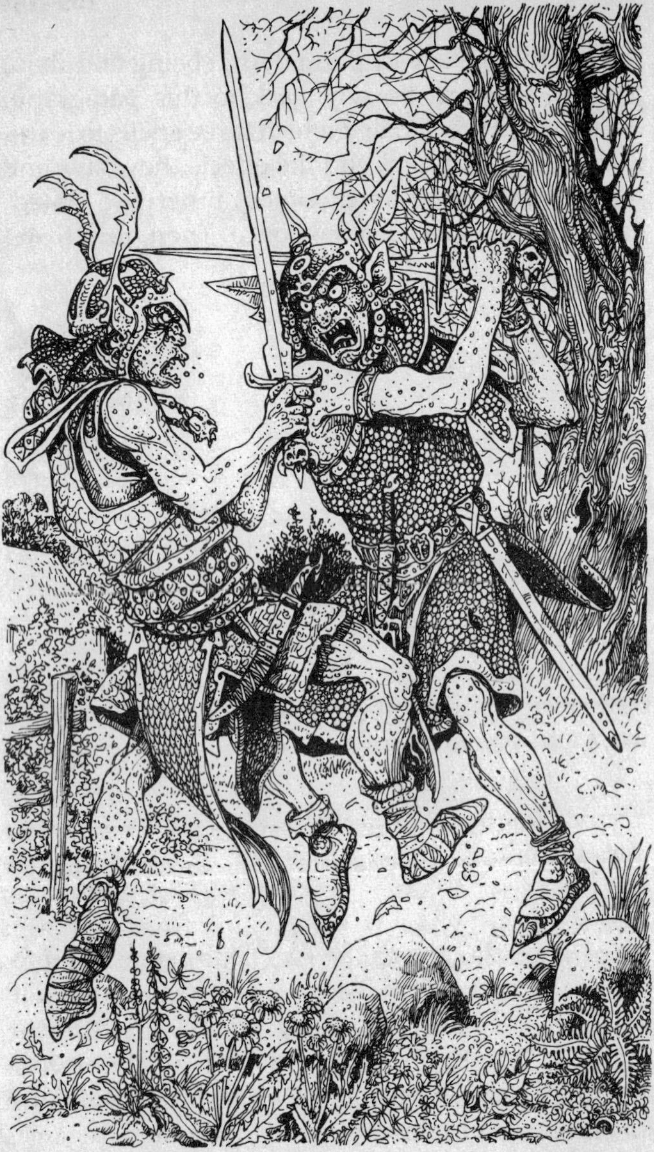

## 191

Ahead, you catch a glimpse of a wooden cottage nestling among some trees – but you are also sure you can hear the sound of clashing metal! As you stand and watch, two Hobgoblins appear from behind the cottage. They're fighting each other! Will you:

| | |
|---|---|
| Leave them to it and retrace your steps back south? | Turn to **250** |
| Move in and attack them? | Turn to **87** |
| Stay where you are and try to keep out of sight? | Turn to **311** |

## 192

In your sleep you have a peculiar dream, which you recall vividly when you wake up. In the dream you are standing before a stone statue of a man; as you look at it, wisps of smoke pour from its mouth and form a skeletal shape which strikes at you with yellowed claws. But a pure white light shines from the medallion around your neck, and you realize the thing is merely an illusion. One blow from your sword destroys it and it is but a harmless small cloud of smoke. You know this is a good omen; regain 1

LUCK point. When you set off again the next morning, you can either head east to the trail and then set off north-west again (turn to 339) or open the trapdoor and see what is below (turn to 157).

## 193

You retrace your steps towards the east, ignoring the way back – there's no escape in that direction, so you press on further east. Turn to 285.

## 194

As you make your way back down the corridor, thick black smoke swirls towards you, and you smell the choking, reeking fumes. You rush back into the Troll's room and slam the door shut to keep the smoke out. Now, you can either search the room (turn to 130) or open the eastern door (turn to 260).

## 195

A spear hurtles out from the trap within, and you suffer a grazing cut. Deduct 2 STAMINA points. The noise of the spring firing the spear, and the sound it makes as it strikes the door opposite, are loud, and you think you can hear noises coming from the north, so you head off south smartly! Turn to 283.

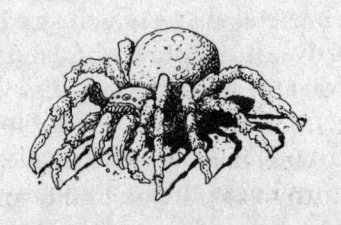

## 196

'Oh, right, Urzak sent you. Well, your instructions are simple. The prisoner is being troublesome and the Master wants the information out of him – how he's learnt to use magic down here without being taught by the Master himself. Get him to talk today and, if he won't, kill him off, very nastily indeed if at all possible. You know the way.' You realize he has taken you for a torturer come to deal with a prisoner! Will you:

| | |
|---|---|
| Attack the young man? | Turn to 3 |
| Open the west door of the dining room and leave? | Turn to 17 |
| Say you don't know the way, and ask for directions? | Turn to 320 |

## 197

You follow the red passage, and the air soon begins to grow hot. You are sweating, and even if you try to turn back, you remain in this wretched place; there seems to be no way of escape. You enter a long red chamber, and in the distance you see an orange passage. It is becoming very hot indeed, and you are beginning to feel faint. Do you have a Bronze Ring? If you do, turn to **263**. If you don't, turn to **32**.

## 198

As the Spider approaches you, a Staff of Light appears in the air before it, connected by a thin luminous thread to your headband. The Spider shrinks back; the Staff whirls into a vortex of light and surrounds the Spider, dissolving it into a pall of reeking black smoke. Turn to **269**.

## 199

You successfully cast your 'Speed' spell; but just as you finish doing this, Mordraneth's spell hits you; a ball of lightning crackles and spins through the air and strikes you. Deduct 4 STAMINA points. But at least you're running very fast now and Mordraneth won't be able to hit you so easily when you get into a swordfight! Will you take the left-hand set of steps up to the balcony (turn to **384**) or the right-hand set (turn to **142**)?

## 200

Your nerves are steadied after you have cast the 'Dispel Fear' spell, and the whisperings and faint cries do not affect you. You step forward, taking care to test your steps, and soon you see faint patches of coloured light which are passageway entrances. You can follow either the brown passage (turn to **362**) or the grey passage (turn to **112**).

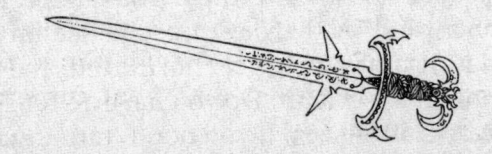

## 201

The Ebony Key slips silently into the keyhole, and the door opens slightly. Beyond, there is nothing but pitch-darkness, and you must have a light source to see by. You can either enter the room (turn to **392**) or return to the main passage and open the door at the end of it (turn to **124**).

## 202

The southernmost door in this room flies open, and a cowled figure stands framed in the doorway. A livid blue scar bisects the left side of his expressionless face, and he waves his thin, almost skeletal, long-nailed fingers as he chants a spell.

You rush him with your sword. Roll two dice and add 1 to the number rolled; if the total is less than or equal to your current SKILL score, turn to **11**. If the dice-roll total is greater than your current SKILL score, turn to **66**.

## 203

As you step through, the 'wall' behind you re-forms! You do not like the idea of trying to return that way; looking around you, you see you are in a passageway along which you can travel west (turn to **314**) or east and then north (turn to **7**).

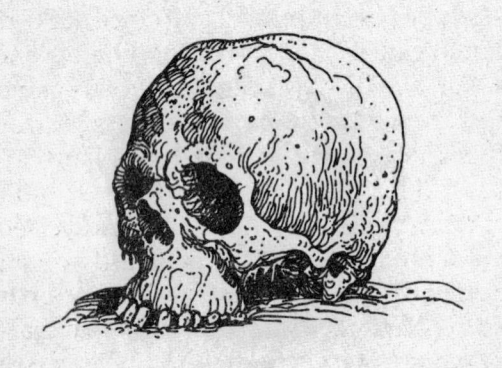

## 204

You open the flask – which is tightly sealed – and a sweet, wholesome herbal aroma fills the air. This is a concentrated Potion of Healing and the flask contains two doses, each of which will restore 4 lost STAMINA points when drunk. You may drink from this flask at any time, except during combats. Add this to the list of Equipment Carried on your *Adventure Sheet*, but don't forget to make a note of the fact when you drink a dose from it!

Now, you must roll one die. If the roll is 1–2, turn to **100**. If the result is 3–6, turn to **156**.

## 205

Beyond the door, a passageway stretches out before you, ending at a T-junction. From here you can go either south (turn to 268) or north (turn to 136).

## 206

You reach the rock face and begin to climb up. It's a tricky, slippery surface, and you curse at the mosses which make it so hard to get good hand- and footholds. Roll two dice and check the total against your SKILL. If the total of the two dice is less than or equal to your SKILL, you make it to the nest; turn to 368. If the dice-roll is greater than your SKILL, you fail in your attempt to climb and fall back. Deduct 2 STAMINA points caused by the fall. If you fall, you can attempt to climb again but each time you try you have to roll two dice and compare the total rolled against your SKILL, as before. If you want to abandon your mountaineering attempt and return south, turn to 119.

## 207

You are fighting a Skull Crab, and you find it isn't easy trying to swing a sword while standing upright in a rowing-boat! You must subtract 2 *temporarily* from your SKILL score. (You do not have to change the SKILL score on your *Adventure Sheet*; this instruction applies only to this combat.)

SKULL CRAB     SKILL 6     STAMINA 6

If you manage to kill the Skull Crab, you pick up the oars again and row safely to shore. Turn to 70.

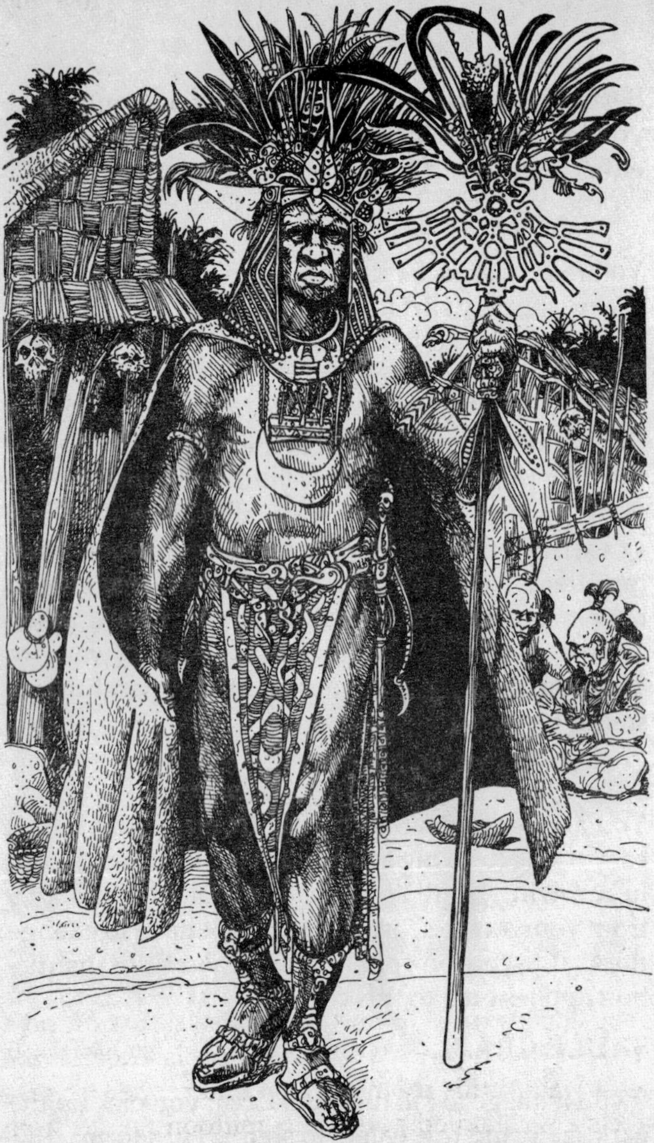

## 208

There are some thirty or so warriors in the village, with womenfolk and shy children who point and stare at you. You begin to feel uncomfortable – but then a richly dressed Native, bearing a ceremonial staff decorated with silver filigree and magnificent plumes, appears from the grandest of the mud-and-wattle huts and approaches you. Haltingly, he speaks in a language you can understand. 'I am Alkandi, High Shaman of the Kiaraboos, and we see you come in peace. You are not one of the Evil Ones. We welcome you with hospitality.' He takes you into his hut, and soon a fine meal is laid before you (restoring 3 points of lost STAMINA).

After you have eaten, the shaman looks at you a little craftily. 'Perhaps some trade between us would bond our friendship,' he says. If you have any Treasure and are willing to trade at least a little, turn to **329**. If you have no Treasure or are unwilling even to consider trade, turn to **258**.

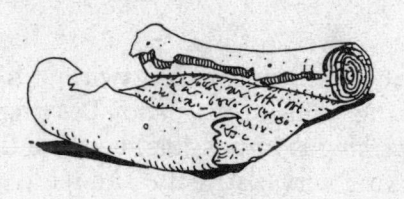

## 209

You enter a room to find three Orcs sitting round a table, drinking and gambling. There is a door in the east wall of this room. As you enter, one Orc projects a well-aimed gob into a spittoon not far from your feet, looks up, and says blearily to you, 'Wozzis? Wanna drink?' Obviously they are not openly hostile, but they do have swords at their sides and there are three of them. You can either attack them (turn to **185**) or sit down at their table for a drink (turn to **359**).

### 210

You try kicking the door down, but it is stuck fast. You also make a lot of noise doing this, and you hear footfalls to the north, coming fast towards you . . . so you set off south. Turn to **283**.

### 211

Inside the foul and filthy-smelling cell, you find that one of the prisoners is already dead. The other, a human, groans, barely conscious; he is clearly very sick. You can try offering him food and water to help revive his strength (turn to **242**), or you can leave him in this wretched place and head back into the main passage and go to the south (turn to **227**).

### 212

He looks at you meaningfully, twirling his dagger handle in the palm of his hand. Leaving without saying *something* is impossible, because the young man is looking very distrustful and ready to attack, and that dagger could fly at your back. Will you:

| | |
|---|---:|
| Attack him? | Turn to **3** |
| Say the people upstairs sent you? | Turn to **196** |
| Say you're a tradesman? | Turn to **60** |

## 213

The 'Speed' spell allows you to run very fast, and also to dodge and weave, avoiding the blows of opponents in swordfights. If you are in a combat, you may cast this spell only at the *start* of it, not once it is in progress. The spell will last only long enough to affect *one* combat. However, during this combat you may deduct 2 from your opponent's SKILL score, because you are so hard to hit! Return to **188**.

## 214

As soon as you attack the Dragon, it disappears! Loud laughter resounds through the huge cavern. 'Well, you're brave, I'll give you that – although you are a fool. I think it's nearly time we met in person, don't you? Enough of these illusions and tricks; *your* soul will give me excellent material to work with. Come along, my puny young fool, along the passage now!'

Mordraneth! Your heart leaps to your throat as you realize the final great combat cannot be far away – or is this yet another lie, another illusion? You can but press on – along the violet passageway at the end of the cavern. Turn to **150**.

## 215

You look carefully around and make out a tripwire, a couple of inches above the floor, in the doorway. Gingerly, you step over it, and as you look up you see the heavy weight that would have fallen on you had you triggered the trap. Now you can untie the old man. Turn to **71**.

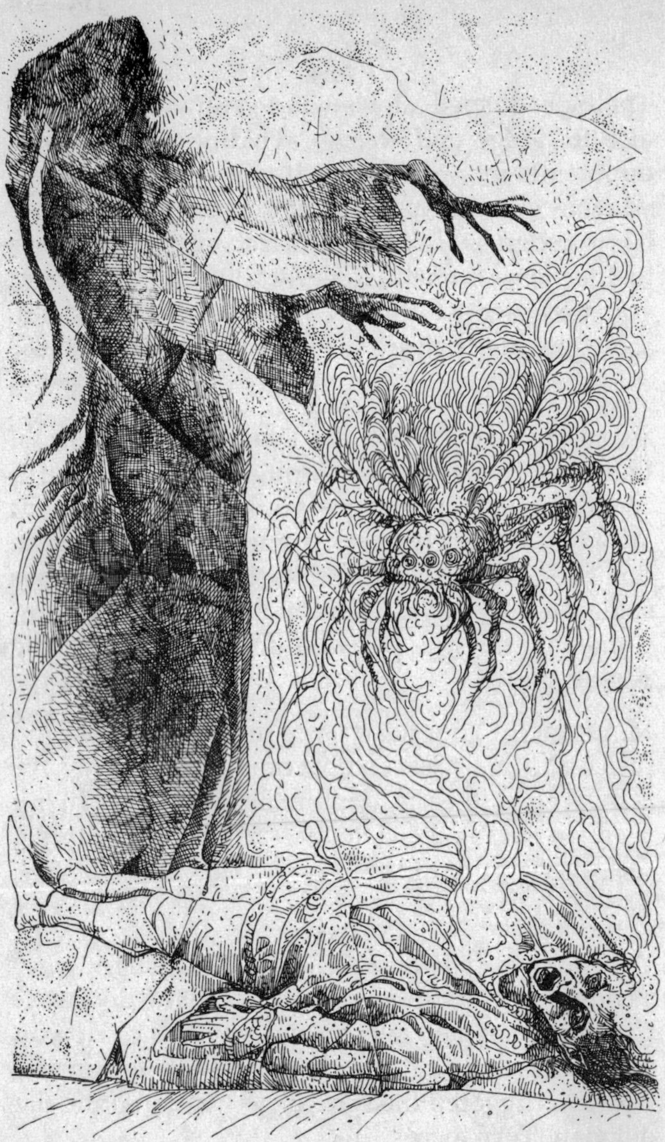

## 216

The carved and scratched marks on the smooth wall depict a horrible scene: a man in black robes stands over the body of an Elf, and his outstretched hands seem to be conjuring something from the head and heart of the body. At first this looks vague, almost a smoky cloud; but as you look more closely you begin to see the outline of a venomous spider with wings taking shape in the cloud. Fully formed, the spider strikes fear into your heart; somehow you know that this is a dreadful enemy! Deduct 1 point from your LUCK. Now, will you:

| | |
|---|---|
| Take the north passage? | Turn to **184** |
| Take the east passage? | Turn to **72** |
| Take the south passage? | Turn to **129** |

## 217

You lose money to the Orcs – roll one die: this is the number of Gold Pieces you lose. If you lose more than you had to start with, the Orcs take your bone dice as well! They drink heartily to celebrate their good fortune; you can either stay with them as they drink (if you do this, turn to **254**) or you can slip out through the door in the east wall (turn to **4**).

## 218

Just a little way past the southern twist in the passageway, you can see two doors next to each other, one on each side of the wall, to the east and the west. Will you:

| | |
|---|---|
| Open the east door? | Turn to **90** |
| Open the west door? | Turn to **358** |
| Ignore the doors and carry on south? | Turn to **283** |

## 219

Roll one die. If the roll is 1–3, turn to **107**. If the roll is 4–6, turn to **75**.

## 220

You sit down at a table with Mehrabian, the half-Ogre; and he pours out a bowlful of rancid, greasy, grey-green liquid in which blobs of a yellow fatty substance float. You wisely decline his offer of a bowl for yourself. He rubs his hands and greets you. 'So, you're the expert torturer, eh? Well, the ole buzzard 'asn't said nuffin', but I 'aven't 'urt 'im too much yet; just a few burns an' such, nuffin' broken. 'Course, I obeyed the Master's command to keep 'is 'ands chained up all the time, to stop 'im usin' 'is magic and suchlike.'

Mehrabian adds a few comments concerning the torture techniques he hopes you'll demonstrate; then he gets up and jingles a bunch of keys he carries on a leather thong at his belt. 'Less go gerrim,' he says, and moves over to a small barred door, hidden in shadow in the north-east corner of the room. You can either attack the half-Ogre (turn to **92**) or wait for him to come back with his prisoner (turn to **383**).

### 221

The snakes vanish! You can cross the chamber safely and take either the azure passage (turn to **272**) or the ochre passage (turn to **77**).

### 222

Your Fire Globe smashes into Mordraneth, for an instant engulfing him in red and yellow flame and a pall of smoke, before he finishes casting his own spell. (Make a note that, when you fight him hand to hand, you should deduct 6 STAMINA points from Mordraneth's total, because of the damage this spell has done to him.) You run flat out up the right-hand set of steps as Mordraneth prepares another spell, and you can almost get to him, but not quite yet . . . turn to **351**.

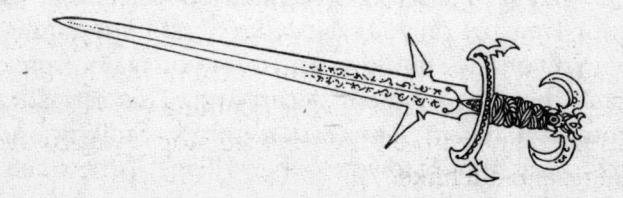

## 223

Captain Garaeth and his men congratulate you on your bravery. You may take Provisions from the ship's galley in order to recover any STAMINA points you may have lost in your combat with the Stormbird. 'Well done,' Garaeth says, 'but this encounter troubles me. It is very rare to see such a bird in these latitudes. Perhaps someone already knows of your coming and has attracted such a creature by magic.' This is not a good thought on which to settle down to sleep; but you get a good night's rest, and in the early morning you feel refreshed and ready to set out for the Isle of Despair. Turn to **143**.

## 224

You give the Natives 1 Gold Piece (subtract this from your Treasure on your *Adventure Sheet*). They smile, pat you on the shoulder, and offer you water from a flask that one of them is carrying. This refreshes you; you regain 2 STAMINA points. Smiling and gesturing, they lead you to their village. Turn to **208**.

## 225

You enter the lamp-lit chamber. Unfortunately, you bump right into the occupant, who was about to set off to bully a few Goblins! You gaze in open-mouthed surprise at each other for a moment, and then you take a swing with your sword as the quick-witted, ugly dark brute of an Ogre sets about you with his club.

OGRE          SKILL 8          STAMINA 10

If you win, turn to **20**.

## 226

As the Troll falls under the weight of your killing blow, he snarls wordlessly at you then croaks, 'You can't get through . . . won't know pass . . .' then he shudders convulsively and lies still.

You look into the room beyond. The Troll's bed, with a table and chair, stands by the south wall, and a massive door of thick black wood banded with iron can be seen in the middle of the east wall. On the north wall there is a plain black cotton wall-hanging which is discoloured by a small growth of green mould at the top. On a second table in the middle of the room are some cluttered items which you'll have to approach if you want to investigate them. Will you:

| | |
|---|---|
| Head back west? | Turn to **194** |
| Search the room? | Turn to **130** |
| Open the east door? | Turn to **260** |

## 227

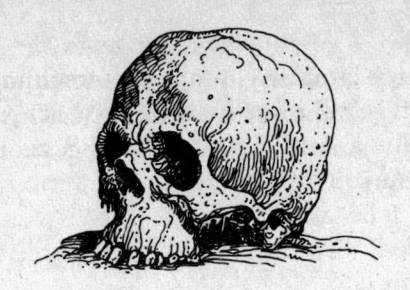

You soon arrive at a door barring your way at the end of this southern passage. You hear no sound beyond, and the door opens easily, revealing light beyond. With sword drawn, you move cautiously through; turn to **59**.

## 228

At the end of the passage is a closed door, the wood of which has many deep marks and cuts from which frayed wooden splinters hang. From outside, you can hear angry cries and the sound of clashing metal on the other side of the door. Do you want to push the door open and investigate the fight inside (turn to **262**) or turn back and head west along the passage (turn to **97**)?

## 229

You find yourself in a circular chamber, from which three passages lead off into the distance. The walls seem to shimmer and shift, as if they were only half-real or as if a heat haze were wavering in the air. The floor feels solid to your feet, but it looks just as half-real as everything else. You must surely now be in the Empire of Illusions, for even the passages seem to shift location, and you have no idea where north and south, east and west lie. Each passage is also of a different colour, unlike this simple, bare, grey chamber. Will you take:

| | |
|---|---|
| The red passage? | Turn to **197** |
| The yellow passage? | Turn to **362** |
| The black passage? | Turn to **149** |

## 230

The Skeletal Illusion advances to strike you down. You must fight it!

SKELETAL ILLUSION    SKILL 7    STAMINA 12

If you win, turn to **381**.

## 231

Your Ring of Fire Resistance ensures that you suffer little damage from the spell; deduct 1 point from your STAMINA. Now you race up to the balcony! Turn to **110**.

## 232

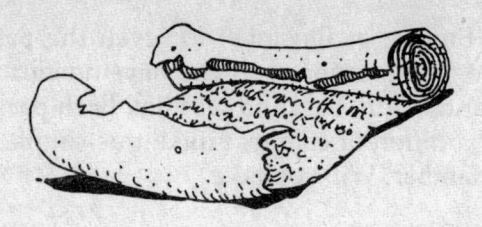

The feather is of no use against the swarming biting rats. Lose 1 STAMINA point because you have been bitten while wasting time retrieving the feather. You realize your blunder and run away; turn to **251**.

## 233

There is nothing you can do to open this chest. Frustrated, you stride out of the room and make your way to the door at the south end of the main passage, and open it. Turn to **124**.

## 234

The blocks of incense will fit into this burner which you may carry with you; except during a combat, you can burn a block at any time (remembering to subtract a block from the list of Equipment Carried on your *Adventure Sheet* when you do this). Each block of incense is a magical block of Incense of Blessing and, when you burn it and inhale the fumes, you will regain 3 STAMINA points. Turn to **305**.

## 235

The Birdman shakes his head sadly; your gift is no use to him. Turn to **322**.

## 236

After your triumph over the Skeletal Warrior, you take a quick look around. The chamber is very bare, lacking anything of interest, so you take the steps down. These steps twist and turn as they descend, but there are burning wall-bracketed torches to light your way. At last, you emerge at an archway cut into the wall of a chamber; you think that this is the north wall, but you cannot be certain. Pausing, you hear no sound, so you step into the room. Turn to **52**.

## 237

Do you have a silver medallion? If you do, turn to **192**. If you don't, turn to **9**.

## 238

You trudge on; the light begins to fail. Not far away, you make out a small cave in the hills to the west of the path. It's too dangerous to sleep out in the open, so you approach the cave carefully and move in. It looks empty, so you light your lantern and peer into the gloom. The floor is littered with rocks, but not too wet. Do you want to settle down to sleep immediately (turn to **337**) or check under the rocks on the floor first (turn to **159**)?

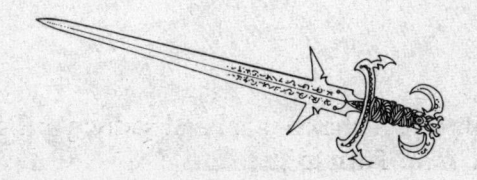

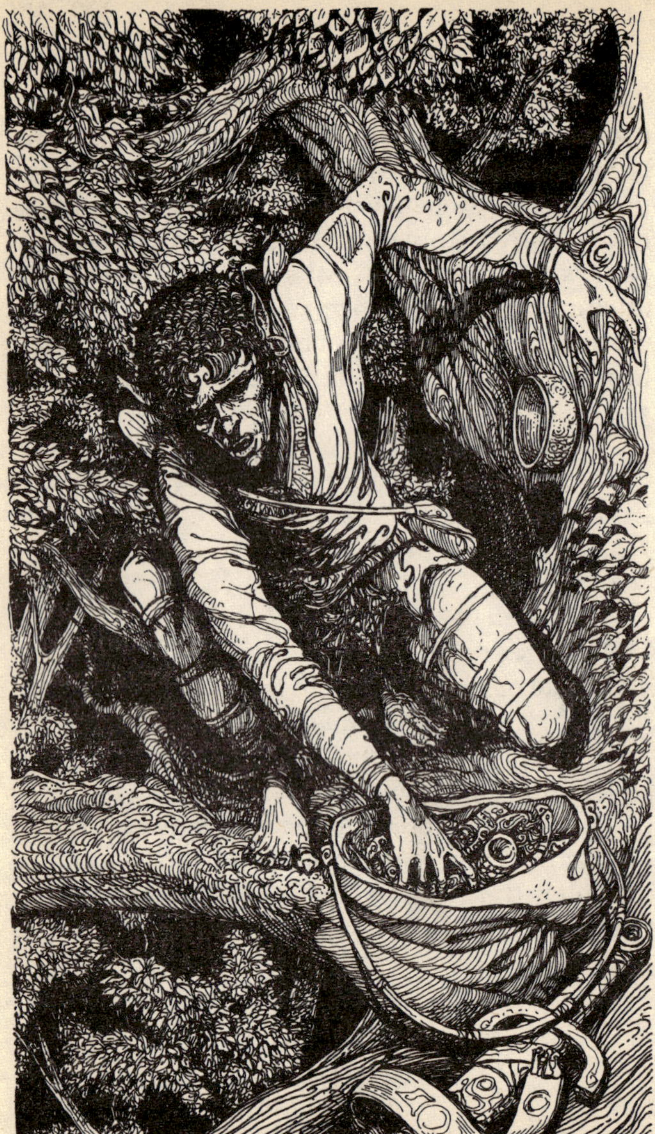

## 239

You are awakened by the Sprite rummaging through your backpack! Angrily you grab him and put a stop to his thievery. He whimpers and begs you to spare his life; he even offers you magic if you will let him go. Do you want to break the little pest's neck (turn to **278**) or tell him that you might spare his life after all (turn to **39**)?

## 240

You are now fighting a huge, angry Sea Giant, and you're in big trouble!

SEA GIANT        SKILL 10        STAMINA 17

If you win, you can go west along the trail (turn to **257**) or north, in the direction the giant came from (turn to **182**).

## 241

As your final lunge destroys the Skeleton Man, its bones fall in a heap to the ground. From the skull a plume of black smoke arises, taking the shape of a grinning vaporous rat! Red glowing eyes form and glare balefully at you. Then the smoke-wraith floats down to the floor and passes right through it! Unnerved by this, you pause to compose yourself then continue south. Turn to **156**.

## 242

You give the man some food and water (deduct 1 from your Provisions total) and he seems to revive briefly. He is still very ill, but at least your kind act makes him more comfortable, and he whispers a few words: 'Orcs . . . guards . . . south. You could surprise them . . . secret door in west before their door . . . but later, beyond, evil . . .' and then he is too weak to say more. He coughs horribly, and his last act is to point at a part of the wall behind him before, with a final gasp, he expires. You remain a few seconds in deep thought over the corpse.

Looking at the wall where he pointed, you observe one slightly loosened brick which is out of reach of the chained prisoners. Will you:

| | |
|---|---|
| Investigate the loose brick? | Turn to **178** |
| Go back to the southern passage and investigate the door at the end of it? | Turn to **227** |
| Go back to the southern passage and look for the secret door the man mentioned? | Turn to **98** |

## 243

Too late, you realize that the Troll must have meant a pass*word* when he spoke his last few words . . . the way through the eastern door must be blocked by magic – and you can't get through it! Worse, smoke is now billowing into the room, and as you look into the cloud of smoke you can see that the acid fumes are already eating away the body of the Troll! If that is what the smoke can do to a Troll, imagine what it will do to you! Now you must *Test your Luck*. If you are Lucky, turn to **146**. If you are Unlucky, turn to **271**.

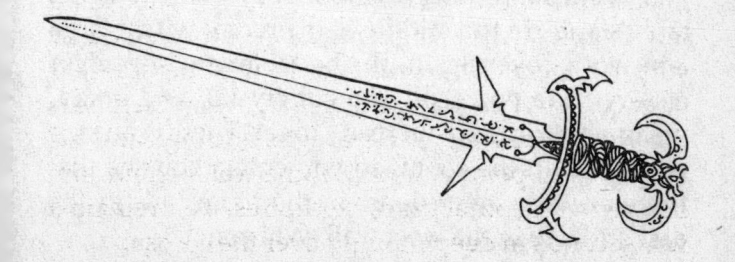

## 244

Since you and Mordraneth are both spellcasting, you must first roll two dice for each of you, then add your respective SKILL scores (Mordraneth's SKILL score is 10), to determine the Attack Strength for both of you. Re-roll any tied scores. If you have the higher Attack Strength during this Attack Round, turn to **199**. If Mordraneth has the higher Attack Strength, turn to **78**.

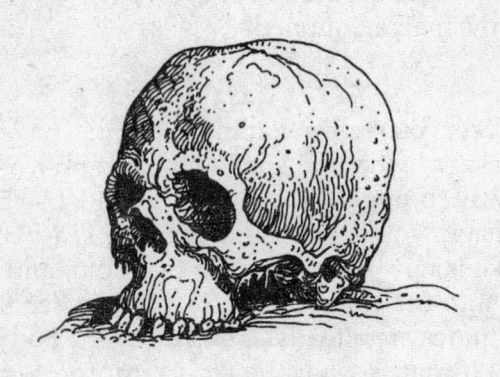

## 245

You follow the passageway beyond the door until you come to another door. This is slightly ajar, and you peer round it into the room beyond. An oaken table stands in the middle of the room, with a large tablecloth covering it; on the table you see silver cutlery, fine porcelain and cut crystal, and bread, meats and fruit laid out ready to eat! There is no sign of anyone in the room, so you enter. You see that there are two other doors in the room, one in the east and one in the west wall. Will you:

| Sit down and eat some food? | Turn to **324** |
| Open the east door? | Turn to **248** |
| Open the west door? | Turn to **17** |

### 246

You cannot easily open the locked chest without a special item to help you. Do you have an Ebony Key? If you do, turn to **355**. If you don't, turn to **81**.

### 247

You follow the twisting, turning passageway until it ends at a door. You force the door open and enter a square plain stone chamber, which has the statue of a man on one wall and two passages opposite; one is blue, one violet. As you step in, wisps of smoke pour from the mouth of the stone statue and form a yellow skeletal figure which glides across the floor and extends its hooked, clawed talons to rip at your throat! Will you:

| Fight the Skeletal Illusion? | Turn to **397** |
| Run for the blue passage? | Turn to **361** |
| Run for the violet passage? | Turn to **31** |

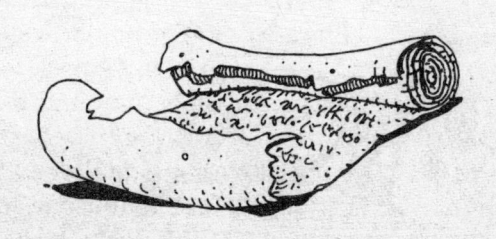

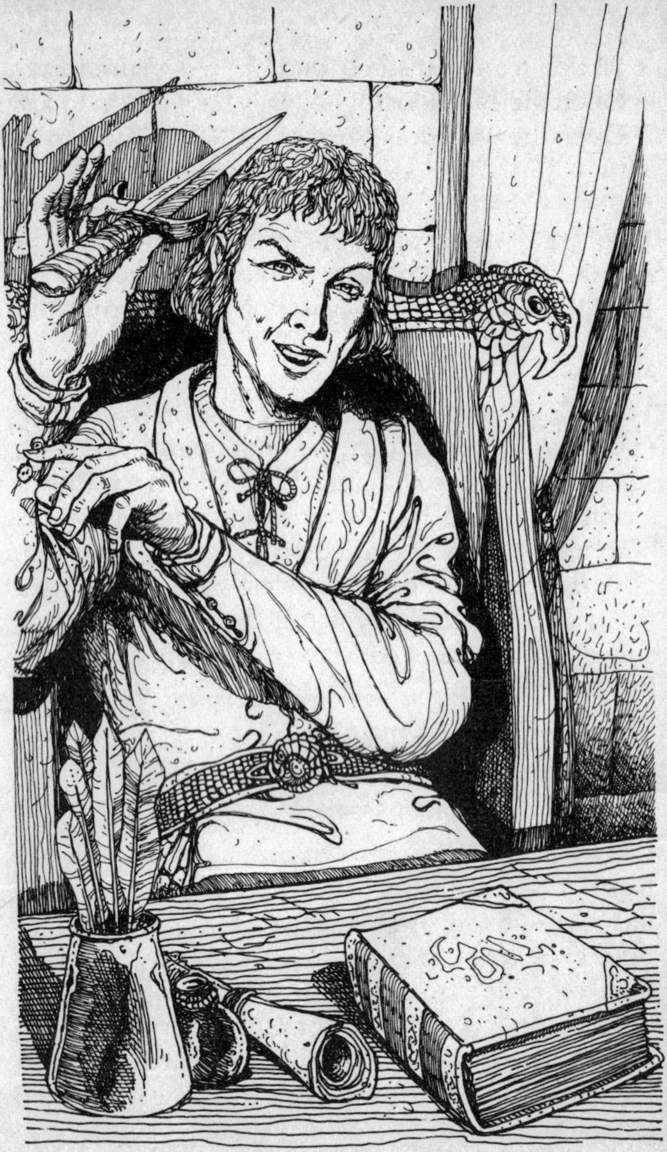

## 248

You open the door into an untidy room with plain furnishings, where you see a young red-haired man sitting at a desk. As you enter, he leans back and twirls a dagger in the palm of his hand. 'You might have knocked,' he says reproachfully, fiddling with a cuff-button on his maroon jerkin. He's not making any hostile moves, but clearly he expects a reply! Will you:

| | |
|---|---|
| Attack the young man? | Turn to **3** |
| Say the people upstairs sent you? | Turn to **196** |
| Say you're a tradesman? | Turn to **60** |

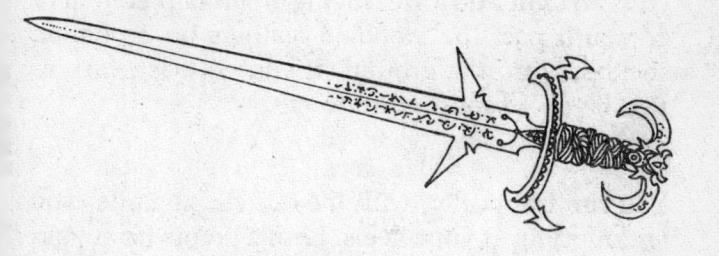

## 249

On this foggy morning, you make out the Isle of Despair, a short distance away to starboard. Captain Garaeth explains that there is no natural harbour here, and you must make your own way from now on. The crew lower a rowing-boat into the water and, taking all your equipment and Provisions, you lower yourself into the boat and row for the shore, as the *Petrel* glides slowly away into the gloom.

You are nearly ashore when a huge pair of grey pincers, trailing green and purple strands of seaweed, rise from the shallow water and snap at your oar! The streaked grey shell, beady eyes and hooked jaws of a giant Skull Crab emerge after them! Will you:

| | |
|---|---|
| Fight the creature? | Turn to **207** |
| Throw some food at it? | Turn to **270** |
| Try to row to shore quickly and get away? | Turn to **22** |

### 250

You make your way back to the crossroads. Now you can either turn west along an unmarked trail or go south past the bloodied feathers on a pointed stick, set into the ground. If you go west, turn to **181**. If you go south, turn to **128**.

### 251

You run frantically, with the rats chasing after you and nipping at your heels. Lose 2 points from your STAMINA through their bites. Turn to **152**.

### 252

The magical bolus wraps itself around your neck, strangling you! Now you must *Test your Luck*. If you are Lucky, turn to **151**. If you are Unlucky, turn to **308**.

### 253

You head on towards the east, and eventually you come to a turning to the south; but only a few yards down it there is a wall of thick, acidic smoke which is too choking for you to pass through. You continue on to the east, then the passageway turns northwards. Beyond is daylight, and you can see a chamber at the end of the tunnel, strewn with rocks and branches. You cannot see anything hostile from where you stand, so you enter. Turn to 354.

## 254

After a short while, all the Orcs fall into a drunken stupor; they are clearly going to be unconscious for some time. Do you want to:

| | |
|---|---|
| Search the room? | Turn to 137 |
| Open the north door? | Turn to 346 |
| Open the east door? | Turn to 4 |

## 255

The passageway winds along, and eventually you come to a T-junction; on the wall facing you is a wall-carving which is rather indistinct. Do you want to:

| | |
|---|---|
| Stop and look carefully at the carving? | Turn to 216 |
| Take the north passage? | Turn to 184 |
| Take the south passage? | Turn to 129 |

## 256

'The nest is just up there, to the north-east,' says the lizard; and indeed you can just make it out, on top of a rocky outcrop. There doesn't seem to be anyone at home, either! Perhaps you can climb up and ambush the birds as they return . . . so you set off for the nest. Turn to **206**.

## 257

You set off west along the trail. Misty drizzle begins to fall, and you feel wet, uncomfortable and miserable. At mid-day you must stop and eat a meal; as you take out some food, you find that the damp has seeped through your backpack and some of your food is spoiled. Reduce your Provisions by 2. Turn to **38**.

## 258

Did you offer a Gold Piece to the Natives you met first? If you did not, turn to **144**. If you did, the shaman regretfully accepts that you have no Treasure left, and says, 'It was generous of you to give my men what you did. In token of this, *I* will give *you* a gift in return.' He has a servant bring him a small silver box which he opens; from inside, he takes out and flourishes an Ebony Key which he gives you (add this to the list of Equipment Carried on your *Adventure Sheet*). 'This was taken from a place below the mountains; it may unlock the way to treasures for you,' he says.

You thank him for his gift, and you sleep well in the small hut he provides for you. Turn to **101**.

## 259

It takes you some time to search through the muck and clutter, and you are weakened by the foul atmosphere. Deduct 2 points from your STAMINA. However, your search is rewarded. You find 2 Gold Pieces the Rat Men had hidden (add these to your Treasure on your *Adventure Sheet*) and also a backpack – taken, no doubt, from some adventurer fallen victim to the Rat Men. Inside it, you find a grappling iron attached to a rotten, useless length of rope which you discard, and a blue silk glove in perfect condition! On the palm you notice an embroidered motif of two intertwined snakes coiled round a staff bearing runes. The glove fits your left hand perfectly, so you slip it on. Recover 1 LUCK point! Add both these items to the list of Equipment Carried on your *Adventure Sheet*. You set off back south; turn to **303**.

## 260

The door won't open! You try forcing it and using the bunch of keys the Troll had, but all efforts are useless. Do you have an Ebony Key, *and* will you use it to try and open this door? If you have the key and want to use it here, turn to **19**. If you don't have it, or would rather not use it, turn to **243**.

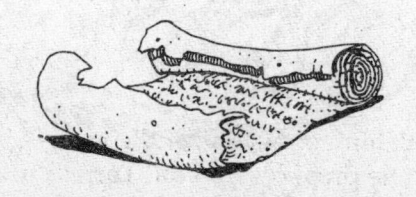

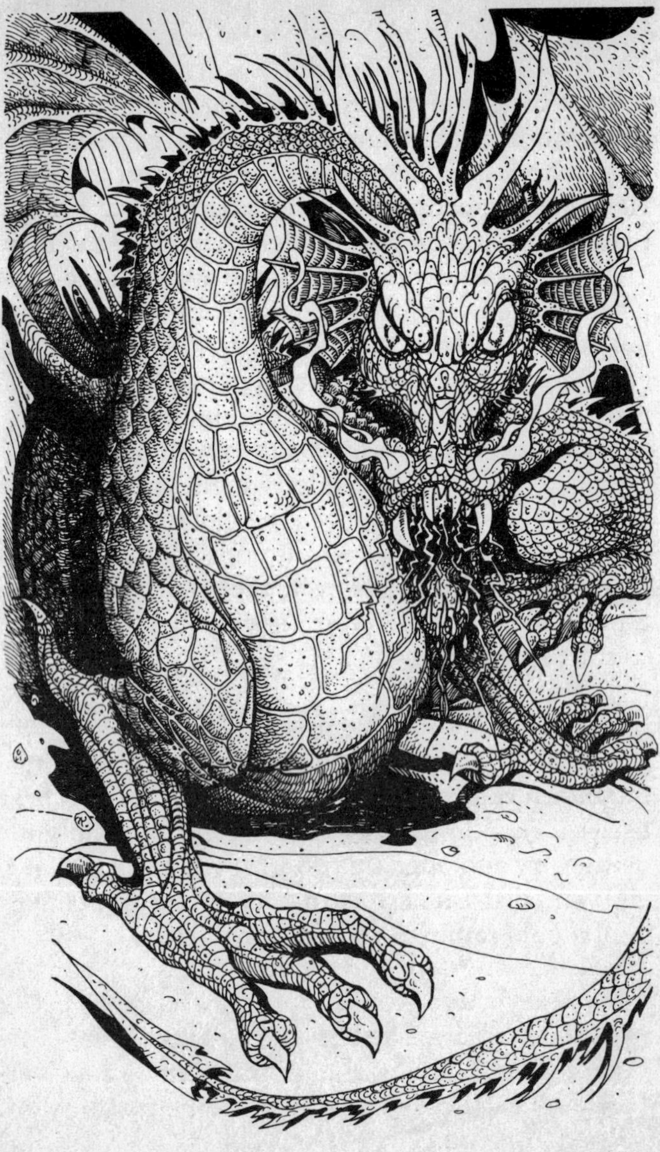

## 261

The blue passage leads down, becoming a steeper and steeper decline. It opens into a huge trapezoidal chamber with a passageway exit in the far distance – and in this chamber sits a vast Blue Dragon! It lifts its head towards you, and lightning crackles in its throat. This is a truly terrifying enemy, and one you hardly expected to see here. It *must* be an illusion, surely . . . ? Will you:

| | |
|---|---|
| Attack the Dragon with your sword? | Turn to 214 |
| Cast a 'Dispel Illusion' spell (if you can)? | Turn to 111 |
| Run back down the passage? | Turn to 341 |

## 262

You open the door and look into a chaotic shambles of a room; crude wooden furniture has been tipped over and smashed jugs and torn papers lie about the place. Two Orcs are fighting each other with swords; each calls out to you for help against the other. Will you:

| | |
|---|---|
| Leave them to it and head west along the passage? | Turn to 97 |
| Help one Orc against the other? | Turn to 148 |
| Fight both Orcs? | Turn to 363 |

### 263

You slip on the Bronze Ring, if you're not already wearing it; while it still seems fairly hot, you're not damaged by the heat. You realize the ring is a magical Ring of Fire Resistance, and you get safely to the orange passage where the heat is less intense. Turn to 362.

### 264

The Orcs have nothing but 1 Gold Piece which one carries in a pouch (take this and add it to your Treasure on your *Adventure Sheet*). Their dirty, lice-ridden chamber smells awful, and you leave in haste; you can either open the easterly door here (turn to 315) or the door to the south (turn to 333).

## 265

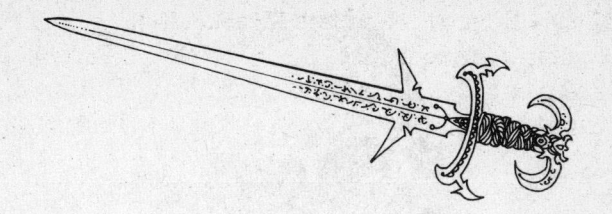

You push open the trapdoor and haul yourself up into a room above. But as you do so, you miss a handhold and, while you get up safely, you make rather a lot of noise doing it.

A light flares in the room as a lamp is lit, and you hear the scrape of metal on stone; an Orc comes snarling towards you, picking up his sword from the floor beside his bed. You get to your feet just in time to fight him on equal terms.

ORC          SKILL 5          STAMINA 5

If you win, turn to **99**.

## 266

After much determined and careful chipping, a skeletal shape begins to reveal itself. You see the glint of metal . . . you must now stop and eat a meal during a break from your work – or deduct 2 points from your STAMINA. Eventually, you uncover most of a slim skeleton – an Elf, perhaps. You can make out the rotted remains of a backpack and a useless, rusted sword, and also a slender flask of white metal. If you decide to investigate the flask, turn to **204**. If you want to leave it unopened, turn to **156**.

## 267

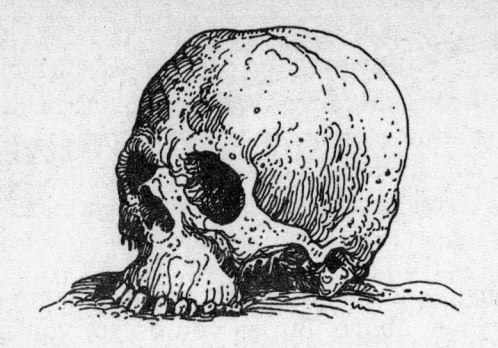

Opening the door, you see a storeroom, full of clutter: half-rotted ropes, a pile of sacking, old wooden staves, and the like. There is also a pile of human-sized skulls on a wooden table in the centre of the room; there might be something hidden in that pile. Will you:

| | |
|---|---|
| Search through the pile of skulls? | Turn to **24** |
| Return to the goblin room and open the north door there? | Turn to **377** |
| Return to the goblin room and open the west door there? | Turn to **205** |

## 268

You head south along the passageway, which then turns west and opens into a chamber lit with flaming braziers. Standing in the doorway, you can just make out steps that lead upwards at the far end of this chamber, and a large stone statue standing before them. The statue, sculpted in stone, is nearly ten feet tall, and has the head of a horned bull atop a man's body. It is not moving and, as you creep into the chamber, it does not react to you. Your heart beats strongly as you enter – will the statue attack? To find out, turn to **366**.

## 269

You stumble across the rocky chamber and into the passageway beyond. Stone steps lead up to a well-lit chamber – the lair of Mordraneth himself, you guess. You stride into this huge, palatial chamber, resplendent with stone pillars, statues and wall-hangings, and lit by flaming braziers; you stand in a hallway with a balcony at the far end and stone steps on either side of you leading up to that raised area. On the balcony stands Arch-mage Mordraneth himself, tall and dark, dressed in flowing black robes. A trace of crystalline dust glitters as it falls from his hands to the floor, and he mutters an incantation – he is going to attack you with a spell! Will you:

| | |
|---|---|
| Cast a 'Speed' spell (if you can)? | Turn to **244** |
| Cast a 'Fire Globe' spell (if you can)? | Turn to **94** |
| Race up the left-hand set of stone steps? | Turn to **332** |
| Race up the right-hand set of stone steps? | Turn to **63** |

### 270

You throw some food towards the crab, which grabs at it and misses. You now have time to row away while the dim-witted crab finds and gobbles down the food. Reduce your Provisions by 1. You row to the shoreline without further incident; turn to **102**.

## 271

You panic, looking desperately for a way out, but you can find none. You hammer at the eastern door, but your attempts grow more feeble as the acid smoke thickens and envelops you. You slump to the ground . . . and in a few hours your body will be nothing more than a pile of gleaming white bones. Your quest ends here.

## 272

You stride along the azure passage, and you come to a bridge over a deep, blue-tinged rock-chasm. You carefully test the solidity of the bridge before walking across it. On the other side is a black tunnel lit with gouts of red light which emanate from some distant fiery source. Filled with foreboding, you head for the dark tunnel, for this is the only exit. Turn to **296**.

## 273

You help the wizard to a chair and unlock his chains, if you haven't already done so. You must give him either something to eat (subtract 1 from your *Provisions* on your *Adventure Sheet*) or a magical 'potion of healing', for he is very weak. Turn to **140**.

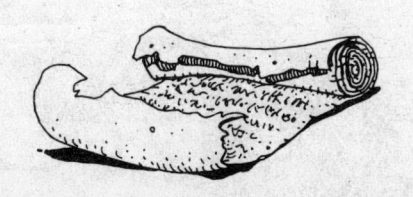

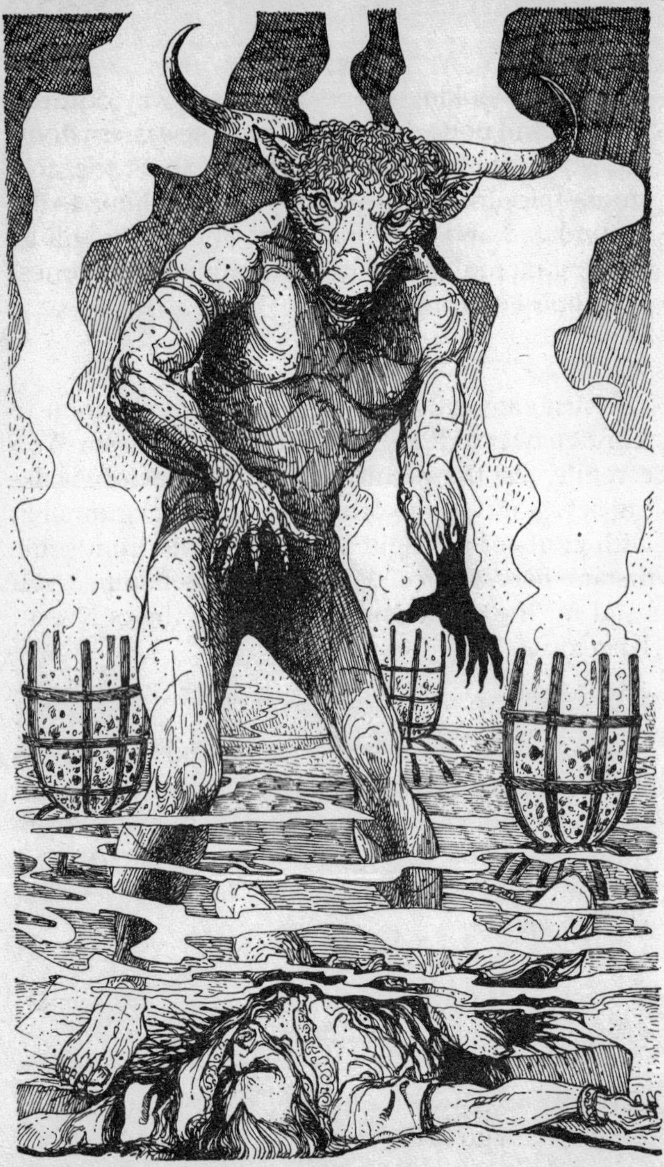

## 274

Soon you encounter a small turning south off the main passage; looking along it, you see steps descending to a chamber lit by burning braziers. Within it stands a massive stone statue of a bull-headed man, motionless above the body of an Elf it has ripped almost in two! Avoiding this horror, you press on along the passage, which heads west and then turns south; turn to **218**.

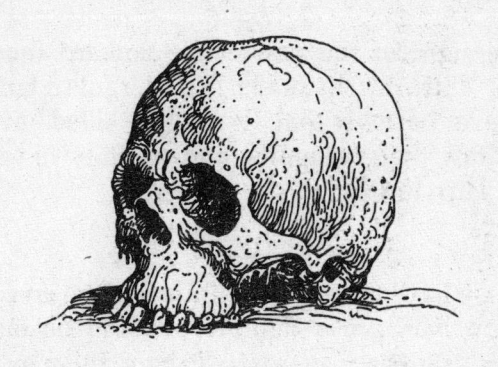

## 275

The Ebony Key doesn't fit the lock, worse luck. Will you:

| | |
|---|---|
| Try using the bunch of keys, if you have them? | Turn to **74** |
| Try using the phial of white oil, if you have it? | Turn to **138** |
| Give up and try the west door? | Turn to **358** |
| Give up and go to the south? | Turn to **283** |

## 276

At the sight of the pewter ale tankard the Orcs freeze. ''Struth! That's ole Thunderguts's tankard! 'E'd never part wiv that! 'E must uv killed 'im!' The Orcs draw their weapons, and you'll have to fight them. Turn to **185**.

## 277

You may have found the entrance to the crypt, but the iron bars are a definite physical obstacle to further progress! You can try to bend them by sheer strength if you wish (if you try this, turn to **40**); alternatively, you can just wait, keeping out of sight, to see if anything comes along (turn to **104**).

## 278

You grip the Sprite's neck in your powerful hands. As you do, a tiny silver charm about his throat breaks and tiny shards of metal fly out and lacerate your hands. Deduct 1 point from your SKILL and 2 points from your STAMINA. Turn to **103**.

## 279

Your sleep is disturbed by an awful nightmare in which you are standing on a path above a sheer rock crevasse, fighting for your life. Flying around you, striking with its bloodied jaws, is a black skull, its eyes afire with an evil crimson glow. You feel with horror its hunger for your soul, as it seems to draw terrors and fears from within you as if to give them substance and make them real . . . You wake up sweating. Lose 3 STAMINA points. Although it's early morning, you cannot get back to sleep after this, and so you may either get back to the trail leading north-west (turn to **339**) or open the trap-door in the floor and explore what lies below (turn to **157**).

## 280

You open the west-side door and stride along the passageway beyond. It is darker here, and you must use your lantern to light your way. The air grows very damp and ahead you see that the passage leads into a long, fairly narrow cavern. To get across, you have to wade through a pool in the middle of it;

testing the water depth, you step cautiously across. However, when you're barely half-way across, an albino aquatic Cave Snake rears its head out of the water and strikes at you! You have to fight it at once, up to your waist in water and while trying to hang on to your lantern – which isn't easy. For this combat, you must *temporarily* lose 2 SKILL points. (*Don't* make any changes to your SKILL score on your *Adventure Sheet*; this is only a temporary change.)

CAVE SNAKE      SKILL 6      STAMINA 7

If you win, turn to **330**.

## 281

You find the secret door Alsander told you about without difficulty, and quietly push it open. The smooth passageway beyond is dark, but you can see light streaming from a gap under a door at the end of it. You move slowly up into position and kick the door open, hoping to surprise your enemies. You glimpse a richly furnished room, and the glint of gold and silk and fur catches your eye, but you have no time to take in details. The Dark Elves inside are too agile and swift to be surprised, and now you must fight them. Fight the Dark Elves one at a time as you stand in the doorway.

|  | SKILL | STAMINA |
|---|---|---|
| First DARK ELF | 8 | 6 |
| Second DARK ELF | 7 | 5 |

If you win, turn to **96**.

## 282

You can either search the room the guard was occupying (turn to **132**) or leave through the west door of the dining room (turn to **17**).

## 283

It is dark to the south, and you must have a light source to see by (your lantern or a Magical Sword if you have one!). Your footsteps crunch on chips of stone, and as you look down you see other footprints leading this way! Vigilantly, you walk quietly on. Soon you see a small side-passage to the east which ends at a wooden door with a small iron grille in it. You can investigate this door (turn to **131**) or continue south (turn to **227**).

## 284

You come to a T-junction in the dark passages, and you see gleams of light to both east and west. Will you go westwards (turn to **154**) or eastwards (turn to **7**)?

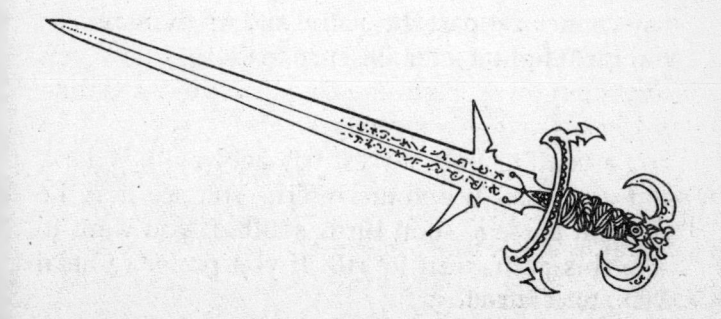

## 285

There is a smell in the damp air which grows stronger, the further you walk along: the smell of the crypt, the dread stench of death. The passageway opens into a darkened chamber; even with a lantern, you can see nothing inside it unless you enter. You may retrace your steps west if you wish (turn to **356**) or you can enter the chamber (turn to **335**).

## 286

You cannot get past the statue and up the stairs, so you must fight it after all. Turn to **84**.

## 287

You ascend to an east-west passageway. It is dark, and you must use your lantern. You see that the western passage soon turns south; if you want to take this path, turn to **218**. If you prefer to head west, turn to **106**.

## 288

You search through the nest and find 3 Gold Pieces (add these to your *Adventure Sheet*). You clamber safely down from the nest, to see what reward the lizard has for you.

The lizard looks very pleased when you return. 'A thousand thanks! Here are rewards for you.' It opens a scaly paw and gives you a splendid rose pearl worth 12 Gold Pieces (add this to your Treasure) and a small Silver Medallion on a neck-chain, which has the palm of a hand etched upon it. 'I'm not sure exactly what this is for,' says the lizard, 'but it's some sort of magical protection against evil. I hope it will be of use to you.' You take this and wear it around your neck (add the Silver Medallion to the list of Equipment Carried on your *Adventure Sheet*). To help you on your way, the lizard also gives you a small dose of a potion which will enable you to run quickly without getting fatigued. Thanking the lizard for his gifts, you quaff the potion and speed away south and then turn west to get back on the right trail. Turn to **349**.

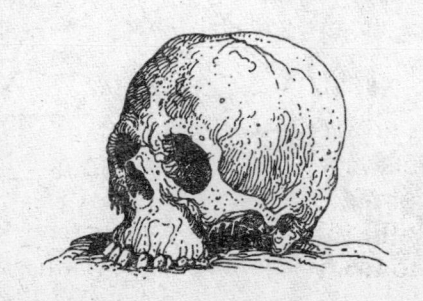

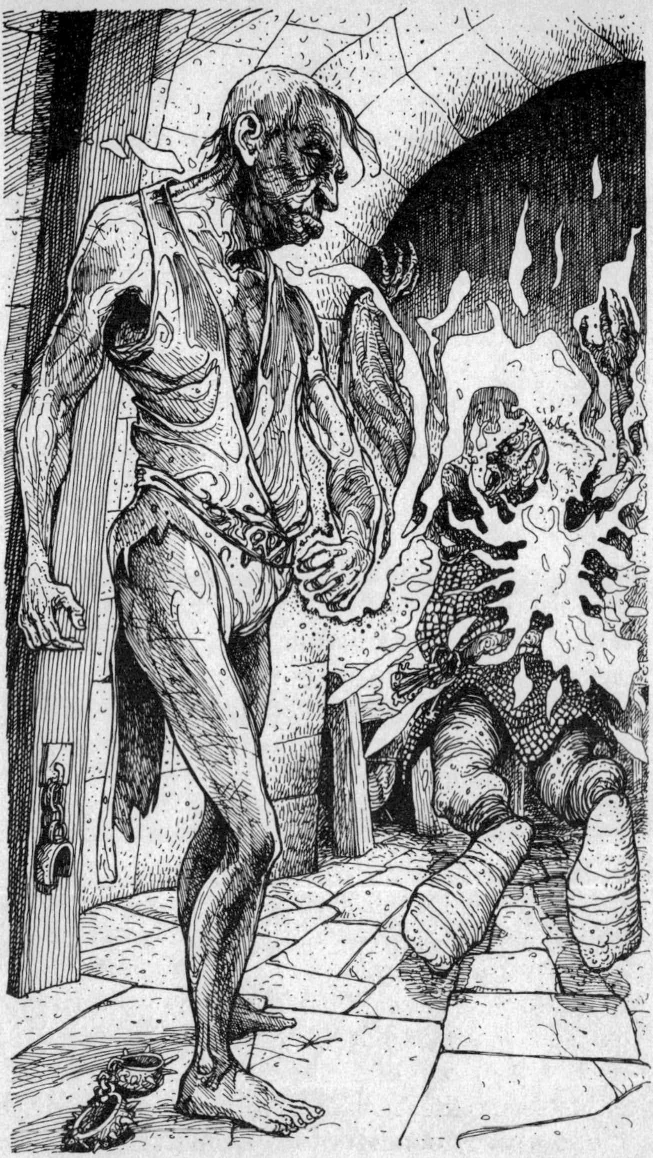

## 289

You slip one of the keys into the lock of the handcuffs and free the prisoner's hands. His eyes gleam with hope as he recognizes you for a friend. 'Step back,' he says grimly, 'I've been longing to do this.' He whispers a few words and conjures a small ball of fire in his hands, then sends this flying through the air; it grows in size and smashes into the back of the torturer, engulfing the half-Ogre in fire and making him scream in pain. The wizard totters back; it's up to you to finish the job he has begun. Turn to **76**. You may deduct 6 points of STAMINA from the half-Ogre's total shown there because of the damage inflicted by this spell.

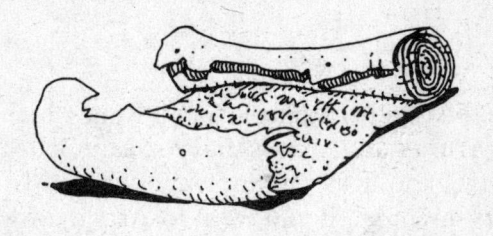

## 290

You creep over and dispatch the sleeping guard with a single blow, slitting his throat. However, this is a cowardly thing to do; to slay a fellow human being so cold-bloodedly – even if he was evil (and can you be certain that he *was*?) – is almost an evil act itself. Lose 1 point from your LUCK. Now, you can either search the room (turn to **91**) or leave and take the southern door in the next room (turn to **245**).

## 291

First, decide how many Gold Pieces you are willing to gamble, up to a maximum of 6 – the Orcs aren't rich and they will probably attack you if they see you have lots of Treasure! After you have decided this, roll two dice. If the total of the dice-roll is less than or equal to your current SKILL score, turn to **89**. If the dice-roll total is higher than your current SKILL score, turn to **217**.

## 292

After the Birdman has flown away, do you want to travel south and west, back the way you came (if you do, turn to **314**), or go westwards along the other passage which leads from this roost (turn to **122**)?

## 293

Inside the chest is a simple Silver Ring which bears strange runes and glyphs that you cannot decipher. You have no way of knowing what this ring's powers might be. If you want to carry it, or wear it, add the Silver Ring to the list of Equipment Carried on your *Adventure Sheet*, then turn to **114**.

## 294

You apply all your strength, and the door splinters in its frame. The effort costs you 2 STAMINA points, but now the door is open. Beyond, you can make out only inky blackness; you must have a light source to see by. You can either enter this dark, forbidding room (turn to **392**) or return to the main passage and open the door at the end of it (turn to **124**).

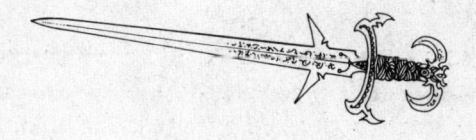

## 295

Among Mordraneth's illusions, some are of fearsome creatures which may appear real to your mind and which you must fight. You will be told whether a 'creature' is in fact an illusion; if this is the case, you can cast the 'Dispel Illusion' spell and destroy the creature automatically. However, you must do this as soon as you attack a creature; you cannot cast this spell once a hand-to-hand fight is in progress! Also, the spell is only completely effective against a *single* illusory creature; if you are being attacked by several at once, then you cannot be sure how effective the spell will be. Under these conditions, you will be asked whether you wish to use the spell and, if you do, you will be told what effects it has. Lastly, if you have the Platinum Amulet, you may use this spell (and *only* this spell) *twice*, rather than only once. Return to **188**.

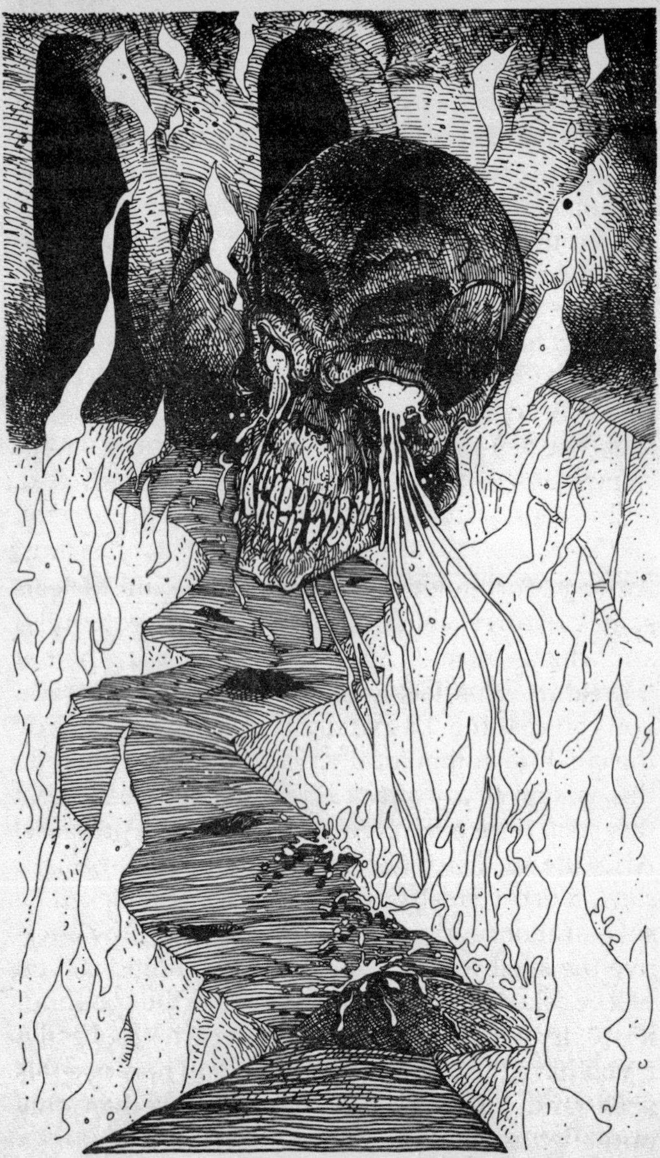

## 296

The black tunnel leads into a chamber crossed by two deep chasms. Gouts of flame spurt into the air from both, and clouds of burning gases hang in the air. On the other side of this infernal place you can make out two passages. You step carefully across the ground, in order to avoid the chasms and reach the passages, but then into the air rises a ghastly thing, malevolent and hideously evil: a jet-black flying skull with glowing red eyes from which blood wells and drips, hissing, into the fiery chasms below. You feel the elemental evil of this thing and its hunger for your soul! You are struck with fear; deduct 1 SKILL point for the duration of this combat, and lose 2 STAMINA points as well. Now you must fight this thing, which is no illusion!

DEATH SKULL       SKILL 9       STAMINA 10

If you win, turn to **15**.

## 297

Mordraneth's Fire Globe crackles through the air and strikes you before you can finish casting your own spell; your spell is ruined and cannot be used again. Fortunately, with your magical Ring of Fire

Resistance you lose only 1 STAMINA point. You sprint up the left-hand set of steps and nearly get to the evil wizard before he can cast another spell at you – but not quite! Turn to 351.

### 298

Your spell was useless; the walls are closing in fast! You can use an item from your backpack (turn to 45) or run flat out and pray (turn to 396).

### 299

Your greed has overcome your caution and good sense. The bracelet is an evil, magical thing, and it hates anyone less evil than its previous owner. It constricts and crushes the bones of your wrist. Shrieking with pain, you manage to wrench the thing off, but you lose 1 SKILL point and 2 STAMINA points from the injury it has caused you. You throw the cursed thing down, and open the door to the east, to get away from the carnage in here; turn to 123.

## 300

A quick search through the room and the goblin bodies reveals nothing of interest or value save for a pair of bone dice they were playing with. If you wish to take these, add them to the list of Equipment Carried on your *Adventure Sheet*. There are three other doors in this worked stone chamber, and all appear to be easy to open. Will you take:

| | |
|---|---|
| The north door? | Turn to 377 |
| The west door? | Turn to 205 |
| The south door? | Turn to 267 |

## 301

Amongst a lot of clutter – shells and conches and driftwood – you find 5 Gold Pieces in a bag (add these to your Treasure on your *Adventure Sheet*) and enough preserved food (salted fish) for 4 meals. Add this to your Provisions. You head south to get back to the trail; turn to 257.

## 302

He looks over the scroll intently, but then sighs and hands it back to you. 'It is too abstruse for me to scry. Perhaps Alkandi could help you. He is the shaman of the tribesmen to the south. Approach them in peace and they will not harm you; they are good people.' You thank him and, since he looks better now and says he will take very great care in future, you bid him farewell. Add 1 LUCK point. As you are about to set off, you notice the glint of gold beneath the fallen body of one of the Hobgoblins.

You stoop down and pick up the 2 Gold Pieces you missed before! The extra Treasure (which you may add to your Treasure on your *Adventure Sheet*) puts you in good spirits as you set off southwards again. Turn to **250**.

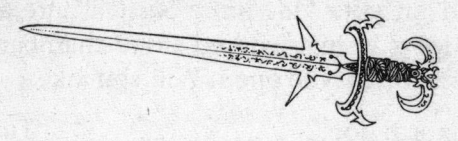

### 303

You set off back towards the south, and return to the junction where the wall-carving faces an eastward passage. Will you take the passage leading east (turn to **72**) or the passage leading south (turn to **129**)?

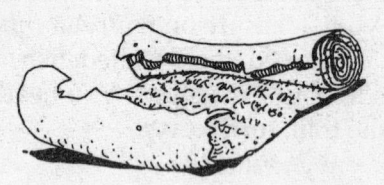

### 304

Hearing no sound behind the door, you open it and enter a small unlit room, which is cool and has shelves on which stand jars, bottles, and some earthenware pots. Checking these, you find that they contain foodstuffs. Most are too disgusting for you to eat (like toasted foot-corn flakeys and smoked dwarfburgers), but you do find a sealed jar of sweet fruit preserve – which would certainly give you energy! If you take this and store it in your backpack, you may add 1 to your Provisions. Now, you may either go back westwards and take the northern passage (turn to **284**), or open a door in the north wall of this small food store and see what lies beyond (turn to **35**).

## 305

You are tired now, and beginning to feel sleepy. Seeing how heavily the trapdoor is barred, and how comfortable the bed looks, you jam the chair under the handle of the door in the north wall of this room (where it wedges it shut splendidly) and settle down for some rest. You sleep well and wake refreshed; recover 2 STAMINA points.

After sleeping, you unbar the trapdoor and look down. Deciding you will have to investigate, you descend the unlit steep stone steps, using your light source to guide your way. Eventually you arrive at a landing; a flambeau blazes and spits green flame on the west wall and illuminates doors in the middle of the east and south walls. Will you:

| | |
|---|---|
| Stay still and listen for noise? | Turn to **27** |
| Open the east door? | Turn to **219** |
| Open the southern door? | Turn to **245** |

## 306

As you sip the liquid, your mouth fills with pain and you spit it out again. This is not water, this is weak acid, the smell of which was masked by the smoky atmosphere! Deduct 2 STAMINA points. Now, you can either open the west door (turn to **373**) or look round the half-open east door (turn to **28**).

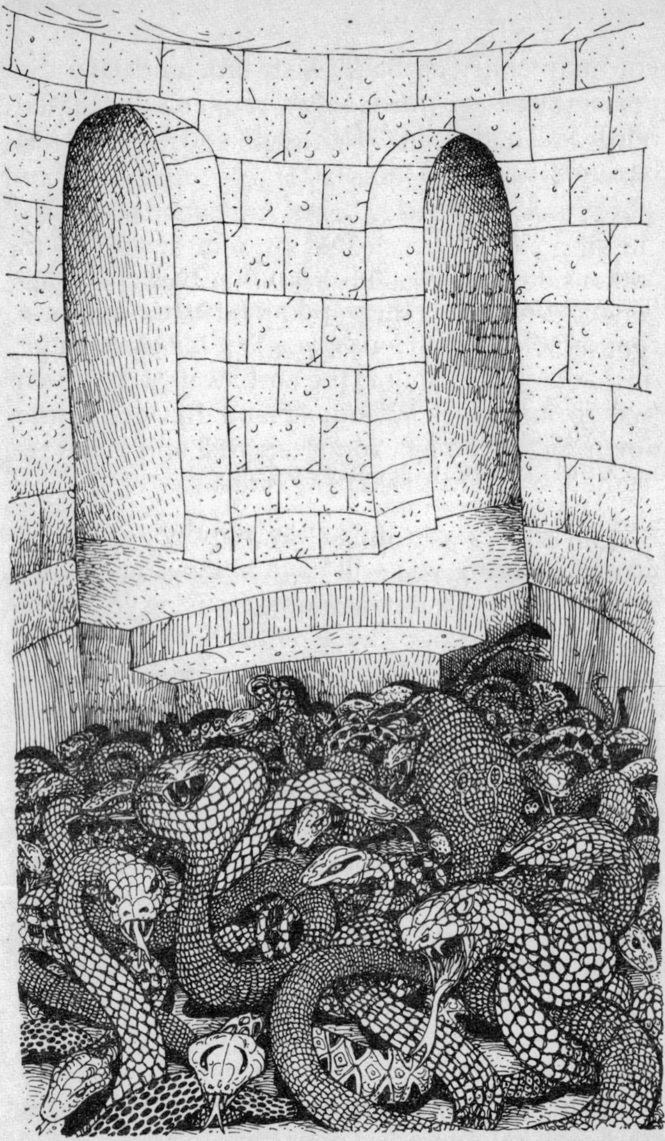

## 307

The yellow-green passage soon opens into a chamber of the same colour with a sunken, earthen floor. Behind you the passage is constricting and there is no way back . . . but this chamber is full of hissing snakes which rear up and sway! On the other side of the chamber you see two exit passages, one of deep ochre and one of bright azure. You must get across somehow! Will you:

| | |
|---|---|
| Cast a 'Dispel Illusion' spell (if you can)? | Turn to **221** |
| Hold out a hand wearing a glove, if you have one? | Turn to **29** |
| Run across the room to the ochre passage? | Turn to **173** |
| Run across the room to the azure passage? | Turn to **109** |

## 308

The entangling bolus wraps tightly around your throat and strangles the life out of you. You feel the Arch-mage's mind probing yours for fears and terrors which he can put to use; as he does so, these terrors and phobias intensify in your own mind, and you are driven into madness . . . you have met a terrible end in your quest for glory!

## 309

You cannot hope to climb the rock surface laden as you are. You may retain your sword, leather armour (but not chain-mail armour!), and any rings you may have, plus a headband, if you are wearing one; but you must throw away everything else you are carrying. Then you can haul yourself up to the top of the rock. Remove *all* other items from the list of Equipment and Treasure on your *Adventure Sheet*! Turn to **62**.

### 310

You will have to fight the two Natives *together*. Each Attack Round, roll two dice for yourself and for *each* of the Natives; add the total of the dice-roll to the relevant SKILL score (either yours or theirs); the combatant with the highest Attack Strength of the three will be the one who lands an effective blow during that Attack Round. Further, if you are hit by one of the native spears, you must roll a die; on a roll of 4–6, you will suffer 1 extra point of damage to your STAMINA from the organic poison which coats the spears.

|              | SKILL | STAMINA |
|--------------|-------|---------|
| First NATIVE | 6     | 7       |
| Second NATIVE | 7    | 6       |

If you win, turn to **21**.

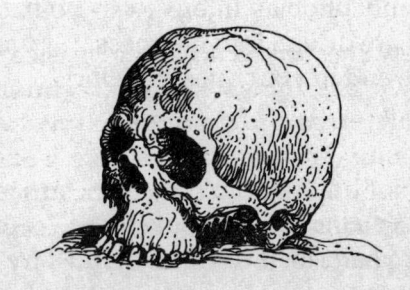

## 311
You must *Test your Luck*. If you are Lucky, turn to **14**. If you are Unlucky, you have been spotted and must fight the Hobgoblins; turn to **87**.

## 312
You fail to bend the bars, and the strain causes you the loss of 2 STAMINA points before you finally give up. Cursing the creature who fashioned the sturdy iron, you decide to stay put for a while and take a rest. Turn to **104**.

## 313
As you put your hand upon the door, an electrical shock jolts through your arm; deduct 3 points from your STAMINA, and also lose 1 SKILL point *temporarily* (until *after* your next combat). Worse, the door disappears – it was just an illusion! As you turn away, you become aware that the stone face opposite is now generating black smoke from its nostrils and that its mouth is grinning! You decide to get away from the foul-smelling, acrid smoke and open the south door; turn to **121**.

## 314
You follow the tunnel west and pass a southerly turning which is filling with black, acrid smoke; you cannot enter it, so you continue on westwards. You come to another turning, this time leading north; although light is shining from it, you can hear a truly ghastly sound as some fiendish thing rips away at flesh and snarls as it does so. You hurry past, and

soon you come to a passageway leading south to some steps; peering down, you see a chamber lit by garish burning braziers. Inside the chamber there is a pile of stone rubble and a shattered statue; beside the rubble stands an intact statue, a bull-headed stone man, with a dead Elf lying at its feet, the torso almost torn in half! Is there nowhere safe in this terrible place? Avoiding these perils, you continue west to a point where the passage turns south and the dreadful rending and snarling noises fade into the distance. Turn to **218**.

## 315

You open the door to a small, cramped bedchamber which contains two lice-infested beds and a pile of stinking, greasy and dirty clothes. Straw litters the floor and a rickety table bears only a pair of evil-smelling dirty socks and a chamber pot. Roll one die; if the result is a 1, turn to **147**. If you roll 2–6, you decide to go back to the guard room and open the south door; turn to **333**.

### 316

With a massive heave, you manage to rip the lid off the chest, with wood-splinters flying and metal bands buckling and snapping. Lose 3 STAMINA points as a result of your terrific exertions; now you must stop and eat a meal after all this work – or deduct 2 more points from your STAMINA. But at least you have opened the chest, so you can look inside to discover your prize. Turn to **153**.

### 317

The gem is of no use here. Lose 1 STAMINA point from bites sustained while you were wasting time retrieving it. Now you see sense and run away fast! Turn to **251**.

### 318

Mordraneth laughs as the Fire Globe smashes into you, causing you 6 points of STAMINA loss. If you are still alive, you keep on up the stairs to challenge his foul sorcery with the cold metal of your sword! Turn to **351**.

### 319

You move cautiously along the passage, but behind you a strong gust of wind almost blows you over, and then the wind grows stronger still! You cannot keep your feet and you are being swept forward by a maelstrom of swirling air . . . your body will be smashed to pieces on the rocks below! Your head swims with vertigo. In desperation, you clutch at an outcrop of rock and hang on, but the wrench to your arm costs you 2 STAMINA points. As you cling on for dear life, a terror of the bottomless drop fills your heart until you manage to control it. Now you must *Test your Luck*. If you are Lucky, turn to **62**. If you are Unlucky, turn to **309**.

## 320

The man looks at you a little suspiciously, but then – to your relief – he shrugs his shoulders and says, 'Urzak's getting forgetful, it must be all those daft incantations he chants day and night. Just go by the west door and follow the passage to the junction, turn right, keep on to the door with the silvered door-handle, go in, and Mehrabian's room is on your left. He'll give you all the help you need.'

You thank him for his help and leave by the west door of the dining-room; turn to **17**.

## 321

You are now in hand-to-hand combat with the evil Dark Priest, overseer of this part of the dungeon, and you will not find him easy to overcome!

DARK PRIEST          SKILL 9          STAMINA 12

If you win, turn to **187**.

## 322

The Birdman speaks haltingly; clearly, he is not able to speak the human tongue very well. In his low croaking voice he tells you this is an evil place and that his people are being driven away by creatures and evil magic, which are taking over the mountain, creeping up from the Iron Crypts below. He thinks they have a prisoner of some importance, but knows no details. He becomes uncomfortable and will say nothing more; and he flies off. Turn to **292**.

### 323

'I repeat the request but once. Give me a gem!' the statue roars. You must either give it a gem, if you have one (if you do this, turn to **8**), or prepare yourself to fight the statue (turn to **84**).

### 324

You sit down at the table and enjoy the delicious food – this replenishes your strength, and you may restore 3 points of STAMINA. However, just as you are finishing your meal, the door to the east opens and a tall, slim, red-haired young man strolls out, picking at his fingernails with a very sharp-looking dagger. He looks at you with some surprise, although he makes no move to attack. He is clearly waiting for you to say something. Will you:

| Attack him? | Turn to **3** |
| Ignore him and continue eating? | Turn to **212** |
| Ignore him and get up and leave through the west door? | Turn to **17** |
| Say the people upstairs sent you? | Turn to **196** |
| Say you're a tradesman? | Turn to **60** |

### 325

'Mordraneth has found a magical way of stealing souls – more precisely, he has found a magical way of stealing the images and emotions of terrifying things from the minds and spirits of the dead. Fear of darkness, fear of death, terror of the dark night when spectres and wraiths roam the world, fear of falling, phobias of many kinds. From these emotional energies and images he creates illusions which have enough power to drive those who witness them to madness or death. He has also found that he gets his best results with the souls of those freshly dead, preferably killed by himself. Hence, he will soon unleash his Illusionary Army on Pollua to wreak havoc, so that he will thus have more souls to steal. I will have to teleport to Pollua to give what warning I can. But it is only here he can be stopped. You are our only hope of stopping him now!' Alsander clutches your arm and gazes deep into your eyes. 'Thousands of innocents will be slain if you refuse to help. The Empire of Illusions is a dreadful place – but I can teach you a few spells to help you there!'

How can you refuse? Your praises will be sung for scores of years, should you succeed!

Alsander smiles, relieved. 'It's fortunate that I learnt a little of how Mordraneth has changed magical forces here, enough to modify some spells so I can use them myself. But time is short, and the Dark Elves may be here soon. I have only the time, and the strength, to teach you three spells before I go, and you will be able to use each one only once.' The wizard walks over to a small chest and puts on his robes. To choose your spells, turn to **188**.

## 326

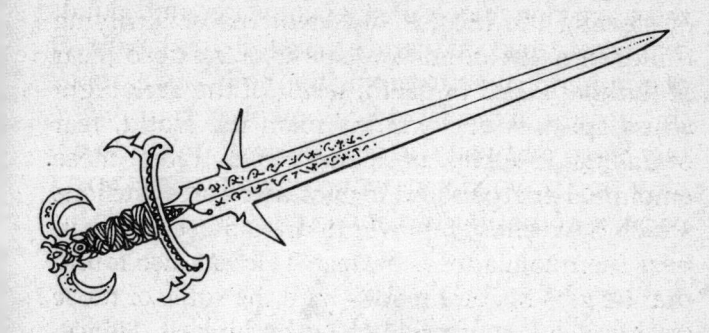

You head north along a limestone passageway, your eyes slowly adapting to the dim light provided by stubby growths of luminous mosses and lichens on the walls. There's just enough light to see by, and you're less likely to be spotted if you don't use your lantern. The passageway eventually bends round to the west and stops at a dead end. But the dead end is suspiciously smooth; as you carefully touch it, you realize that the 'rock' is just an illusion – there is a door here! Keeping your sword ready, you turn the door handle; it gives, so you walk through. Turn to **120**.

## 327

You pass by the skull. As you walk away, a horrid wheezing laugh, as dry as gravedust, follows you. You look around, and see the skull is facing you now, its jaws open in a mocking grin! You move hurriedly away, and soon you are striding through overgrown scrubland and the ground is sloping downwards. You are heading into woodlands;

there are many pools of stagnant water, and clouds of buzzing insects swarm around. If you have a jar of ointment, you must apply this now (and cross off this item from the list of Equipment on your *Adventure Sheet*) and you will be protected; if you do not have the jar, you must deduct 3 points of STAMINA because of the effects of insect bites. Turn to **191**.

## 328

'Sorry about Edwina,' the Sea Giant says, 'she's frisky today. I hope she hasn't hurt you? Good.' He looks around at the mist. 'It's going to rain. Would you care for food and shelter?' If you want to accept his offer, turn to **118**; if you decline and set off west along the trail, turn to **257**.

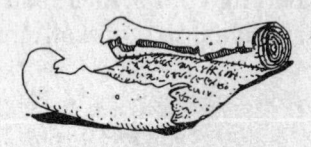

## 329

The shaman has a box brought to him by a servant, then he lays out its contents before you. He tells you the price of each item. You may buy whichever ones you want (if you have the price!); add the items to the list of Equipment on your *Adventure Sheet*, reducing your Treasure accordingly. You can't haggle with him, he's too crafty for that. If you do not have enough Gold Pieces for everything you'd like to take, but you *do* have a rose pearl, Alkandi will give you items up to the value of 8 Gold Pieces in return for the pearl (and no haggling!). The items the shaman offers you are:

| | |
|---|---|
| A silver feather | 2 Gold Pieces |
| An ebony key | 4 Gold Pieces |
| A small ivory statuette of a cat | 3 Gold Pieces |
| A 15-foot length of rope | 2 Gold Pieces |
| A small white gem | 3 Gold Pieces |
| A phial of white oil | 2 Gold Pieces |

You may also buy Provisions here; 1 Gold Piece will buy you enough for two meals – but you cannot buy more than this because the food is perishable and will not stay fresh for long. When you have completed your purchases, the shaman has you shown to a comfortable hut, where you can sleep peacefully, so turn to **101**; but if you buy nothing, turn to **144**.

### 330

You complete your crossing of the pool and set off along the passageway beyond; it is still dark, so you must use your lantern. Water drips from the ceiling and thick hanging stalactites make progress slow and difficult. As the passageway bends to the south, a stalagmite formation on the floor catches your eye; it is clearly unusual in shape. If you want to stop and examine it more closely, turn to **145**. If you want to press on south, turn to **156**.

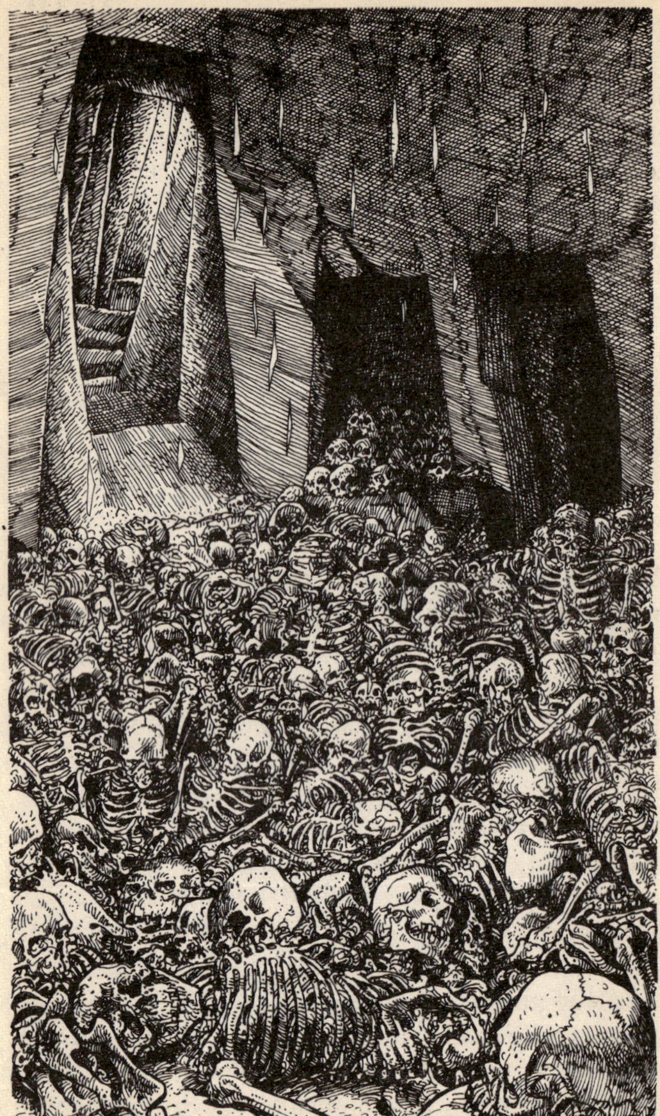

## 331

The icy-cold passage leads down to a veritable charnel-house. In the gloomy chamber, ice crystals seem to hang in the air above a forest of unburied skeletons which litter the cold stone floor. There are two exit-passages not far away, close to where you entered. Will you:

| | |
|---|---|
| Take the light, airy way out? | Turn to 319 |
| Take the dark-brown, earthy exit-passage? | Turn to 247 |
| Stay and say a prayer for the souls of the dead here? | Turn to 134 |

## 332

As you run up the steps, you realize that some magical force is retarding your progress; it feels like running through water! You grit your teeth and struggle on, and you'll get there in the end – but just now a smoking ball of fire is streaking from Mordraneth's hand to strike you down. Are you wearing a bronze ring? If you are, turn to 47. If you aren't, turn to 318.

## 333

A passageway leads south beyond the door, and this is dimly lit by torches in wall sconces. Following the short passage to the end, you see that it soon turns east; however, there is a plain darkwood door on the west side of the passage at the end, facing the east-turning main passageway. You cannot see to the end of that eastern passage yet. Will you try to open the door to the west (turn to 34) or press on eastwards (turn to 364)?

## 334

Making a quick check, you discover a sliding panel in the wall beside the door, and you realize this is where the voice must have come from. You open it and draw out a glowing sword! You take the sword and hurry through the concealed doorway, closing it behind you, and move on up the stairs. However, you have inhaled some of the corrosive smoke into your lungs; deduct 2 points from your STAMINA.

You make your way up a few stairs to breathe the cleaner air, then pause to take a good look at the glowing sword. It is beautifully crafted, of finest steel, with amethysts and tourmalines in the pommel. It does not speak to you again, but it will glow brightly – whenever you will it to do so! Further, this is a Magical Sword; you may add 1 point to your SKILL score when using it, and this *will* allow you to exceed your *Initial* SKILL score (but this bonus applies *only* in combats). What's more, the sword uses power to heal you – after each combat, you may restore 1 point to your STAMINA score if you have been wounded *during that combat*. You cannot take this healing until after a combat is ended. You found a powerful ally in your struggle against the brooding evil of the Iron Crypts! Add the Magical Sword to the list of Equipment Carried on your *Adventure Sheet*. Turn to 58.

## 335

Now that you are very close to the entrance, you can see a round chamber littered with bones. Stone steps leading down into the floor are cut in the far end of the chamber. Turning towards you as you gaze in is a skeletal figure carrying a huge, ice-blue, two-handed sword. You can either flee to the west (turn to **116**) or move in to attack it (turn to **169**).

## 336

The 'Healing' spell is a powerful one which will allow you to recover lost STAMINA. You can cast this spell at any time, except during a combat, and you will be able to recover STAMINA points equal to one-half your *Initial* STAMINA score (rounding fractions down). Return to **188**.

## 337

You must eat another meal before sleeping, or lose 2 STAMINA points. After you've eaten, you unroll your blanket and try to get some sleep. The wind howls outside and during the night a storm thunders overhead, but you snatch a few hours of sleep, enough for you to get reasonable rest. Turn to **10**.

## 338

The Sprite has stolen something from your backpack! If you had up to 5 Gold Pieces, he has stolen all of them; if you had more than 5, he has generously left you the rest! If you had no Gold Pieces, he has stolen your rose pearl. Turn to **103**.

## 339

You head along the trail towards the higher peaks. You soon see that the trail leads to an entrance into the hillside rather than continuing into the mountains themselves. Moving closer, you can distinguish the motif of a skull set into the hillside above the entrance, crafted from iron plaques and spikes! This is obviously the way in to the dreaded Iron Crypts. Excitement runs through your body as you move as silently as you can towards the entrance, sword readied. Edging forward, you observe a passage leading down; there is a faint light from some luminous plants growing on the wet limestone walls, and your eyes soon get used to this, so you don't need to use your lantern. Cautiously, you move along the winding tunnel, and soon you come to a crude wooden door blocking your way. You try the handle carefully, and find you can open it with ease. Sword in hand, you enter the room beyond. Turn to **120**.

## 340

You try to dash past the statue. As you attempt this, it strikes out at you and hits you; deduct 2 points from your STAMINA. Now roll two dice. If the dice-roll total is less than or equal to your current SKILL score, turn to **68**. If the total is greater than your current SKILL score, turn to **286**.

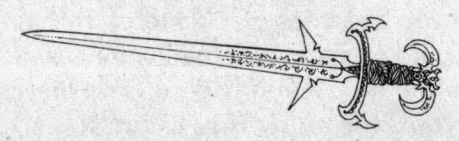

## 341

A massive lightning bolt shoots down the tunnel after you and crashes into you. You scream in mortal agony as pain convulses your body and you smell burning flesh in your nostrils. As you collapse, dying, you feel Mordraneth's magic plucking at your mind to extract the terrors and fears you have experienced in this wretched place. Your torments have just begun, and you have failed.

## 342

As soon as you slay the eagle, the illusion simply disappears, and you find yourself lying on the ground, flailing at the empty air! A low-pitched chuckle fills your ears. 'Welcome to my Empire!' the voice gloats, 'although I don't think you will be here for long.' You see no one, and you find yourself in the middle of a brown passage. At one end, the passageway grows blacker; if you wish to go this way, turn to **149**. At the other, it grows green; if you wish to go this way, turn to **395**.

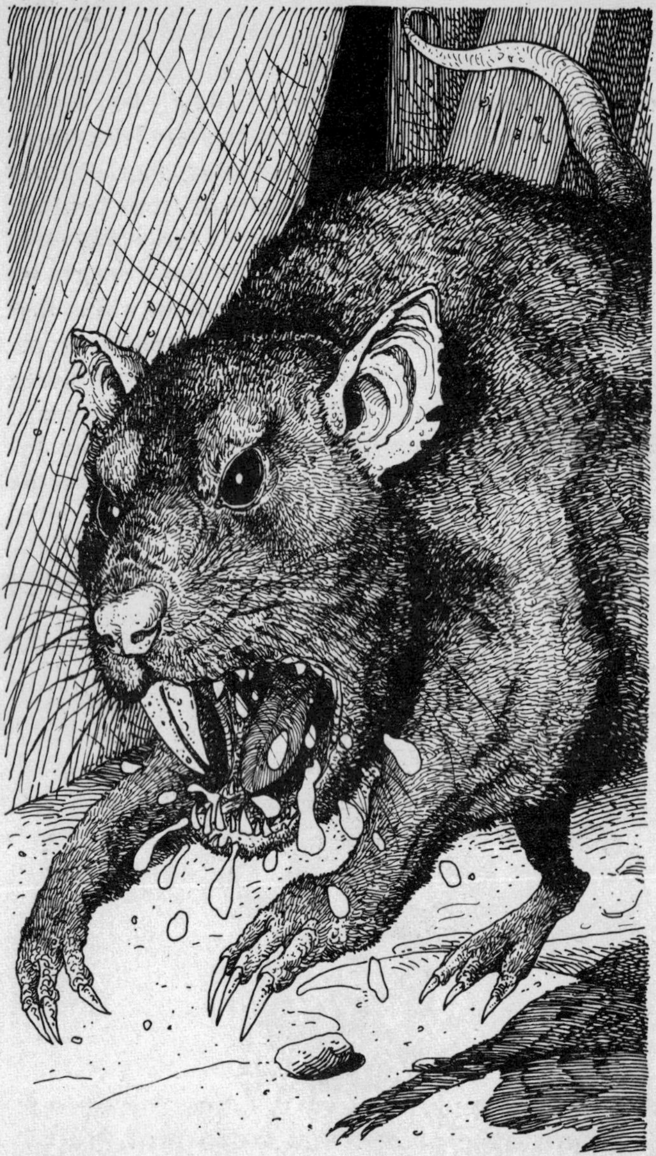

## 343

You find a leather pouch with 2 Gold Pieces on the body of one of the Orcs (add this to your Treasure). However, as you are checking around, Horace, the pet rat of one of the Orcs, nips out from behind some upturned furniture. Horace is a large and very mean rat, and he has a tooth abscess which is making him especially vicious today; he sinks his yellowed fangs into your leg. Deduct 2 points from your STAMINA. To add insult to injury, the sleek rodent scuttles off and hides behind a pile of furniture, and it isn't worth your time or energy to pursue him. You leave the room and head off westwards; turn to **97**.

## 344

You hear nothing. Now open either the eastern door (turn to **219**) or the southern door (turn to **245**).

## 345

Eating strange fungi is not exactly an intelligent thing to do. Within a few moments you're as sick as a dog; deduct 4 points from your STAMINA. You have to sit and rest for a while before you can continue west; turn to **51**.

## 346

As you open the door, clouds of heavy, thick black smoke roll down the corridor towards you. You shut the door and turn away, opening the east door in the Orcs' room. Turn to **4**.

## 347

The ship's crew are glad to see you win – but they also saw you try to run away, and mutterings are heard about cowardice. If you need to eat one or more meals to restore lost STAMINA, you'll have to use your own Provisions to do so, so alter your Provisions accordingly. Turn to **249**.

## 348

You hear a shout and the patter of nasty little goblin feet, then the sound of creaking railings. The goblin has called a friend along, and they opened the gates and now stand before you, their swords at the ready. It is futile to try talking to them, so you must fight them. Fight the goblins one at a time, as you are backed up in a side-tunnel.

|              | SKILL | STAMINA |
|--------------|-------|---------|
| First GOBLIN | 5     | 6       |
| Second GOBLIN| 6     | 5       |

If you win, the gates are open and you can now head along the passageway, keeping your sword unsheathed – there may be more goblins about! Turn to **326**.

## 349

You make good progress along the trail, but as the sun begins to set you see no sign of a safe place to sleep; there are hills to the north, and only the continuing trail in the west . . . to the south there's a small copse of trees nestling against the rock face. You move up to take a look around. As you warily check the trees, a tiny, thin face with drooping, pointed ears and sharp little black eyes peers round a clump of bushes. 'Are you looking for somewhere to sleep?' the Tree Sprite asks shyly. You nod your head, and he races up a tree trunk and fumbles at something out of sight. Then he throws down a rope hammock! 'Get up in the trees,' he urges, 'there might be a wolf about – or worse.'

He dances away through the high branches and is gone. You take his advice, clamber up a tree, rig up the hammock, and settle into a sound sleep. Do you have any Treasure? If you do, turn to **158**. If you don't, turn to **103**.

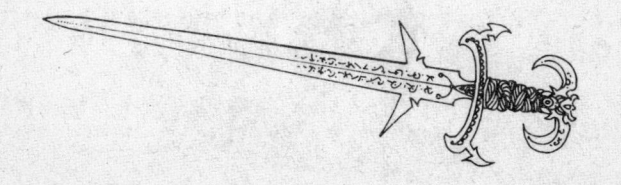

## 350

Alkandi reads the scroll, and a worried frown crosses his brow. 'I have sensed some magical evil in the night-time breezes lately; whisperings of tormented souls imprisoned by an evil creature. This may be the singing which the writer speaks of. I feel also that the spirits of the dead lie uneasy here, that old terrors are awakened by one who has come here. Perhaps this one is the Stealer of Souls mentioned. I can tell you no more, but take heed of the writer's words and beware of singing voices that lure you!' Pondering his words, you set off north towards the crossroads and, once there, you turn west along the unmarked trail. Turn to **181**.

## 351

You still can't reach Mordraneth; as he chants, a whirling bolus of black threads materializes above his head and whirls through the air towards you. Are you wearing a silver ring? If you are, turn to **79**. If you aren't, turn to **252**.

## 352

All the rats vanish! You run towards the distant light. Turn to **152**.

## 353

The Orc has 1 Gold Piece which you may take (add this to your Treasure) but his flask has shattered on the ground and his oil is spilled. The Priest's armour is ruined by a sword thrust, and you'd rather have your sword than his flail. But he does wear a gold bracelet. Will you:

| | |
|---|---|
| Take the Dark Priest's bracelet? | Turn to **299** |
| Look through the south door in the Orc's room? | Turn to **82** |
| Try the door to the east in the Orc's room? | Turn to **123** |

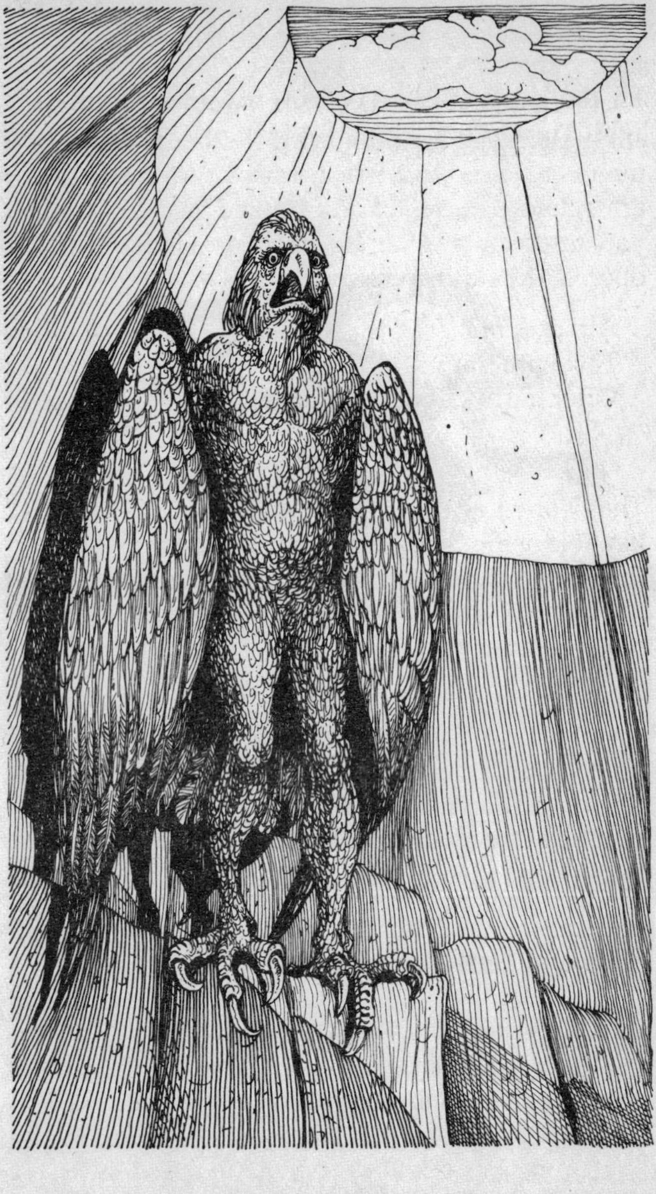

## 354

As you enter the chamber, a figure opposite you stirs: a strange creature with the body shape of a man, but one who has feathers, great wings for arms, talons for feet, and a beaked face. He looks at you suspiciously from his perch on a ledge which is open to the skies. Will you:

| | |
|---|---|
| Attack him? | Turn to **186** |
| Talk with him? | Turn to **322** |
| Offer him a gift of some kind? | Turn to **67** |

## 355

The Ebony Key shrinks a little in size to fit the small keyhole of the chest, which springs open. However, the Ebony Key immediately vanishes! Cross it off the list of Equipment Carried on your *Adventure Sheet*. Turn to **153**.

## 356

As you travel in a westerly direction, a faint singing can be heard on the air, as if a subterranean choir was at its devotions in the far distance. You see that the passage turns north and opens into a vaulted chamber from which the sound seems to be coming. You can either enter the chamber (turn to **36**) or retrace your steps back east (turn to **193**).

## 357

The carpets and furs in this room are valuable, but far too heavy to carry. However, looking around, you find a crowbar in one corner of the room, and you may take this (add it to the list of Equipment Carried on your *Adventure Sheet*). Now you must *Test your Luck*; if you are Lucky, turn to **163**. If you are Unlucky, turn to **139**.

## 358

You open the door effortlessly, but now you must *Test your Luck*! If you are Lucky, turn to **179**. If you are Unlucky, turn to **195**.

## 359

Do you have *either* or *both* a pewter ale tankard or a pair of bone dice? If you do, turn to **105**; if you have neither, turn to **161**.

## 360

You rush the lizard – which simply vanishes before you can get to it! Then a whispering voice pronounces a curse on you for attacking one who meant you no harm; deduct 1 point from your LUCK. You run off southwards in fear; turn to **54**.

## 361

You do not make it before the Skeletal Illusion strikes you in the back. Lose 2 STAMINA points. Then your adversary appears in front of you! Turn to **397**.

## 362

You are about half-way along the passage when you are suddenly snatched up into the air as the ceiling dissolves! The area is filled with airy, yellowish light, and as you float in the air you become aware of a great eagle flying in to attack you. Surely it's an illusion . . . but your senses say it is real, and you can see blood on its talons and beak. You must fight it, and you have to subtract 2 points from your SKILL while doing so (this is a *temporary* loss, for the length of this combat only, as it isn't easy to fight floating in mid-air when you're not used to it!).

EAGLE-ILLUSION   SKILL 7   STAMINA 8

If you win, turn to **342**.

### 363

You must fight both Orcs *together* in this chamber. Roll two dice for yourself then for *both* the Orcs each Attack Round. The combatant with the highest Attack Strength (dice-roll total plus current SKILL) is the one who will get in a successful strike during that Attack Round. Fortunately, the Orcs are both slightly wounded already.

|           | SKILL | STAMINA |
|-----------|-------|---------|
| First ORC | 5     | 3       |
| Second ORC| 5     | 4       |

If you win, turn to **65**.

### 364

At the end of the passageway leading east, you stand before a door marked with a black and amber cross. You can either open the door (turn to **393**) or go back to the west and investigate the door you noticed before, opposite the turning east (turn to **34**).

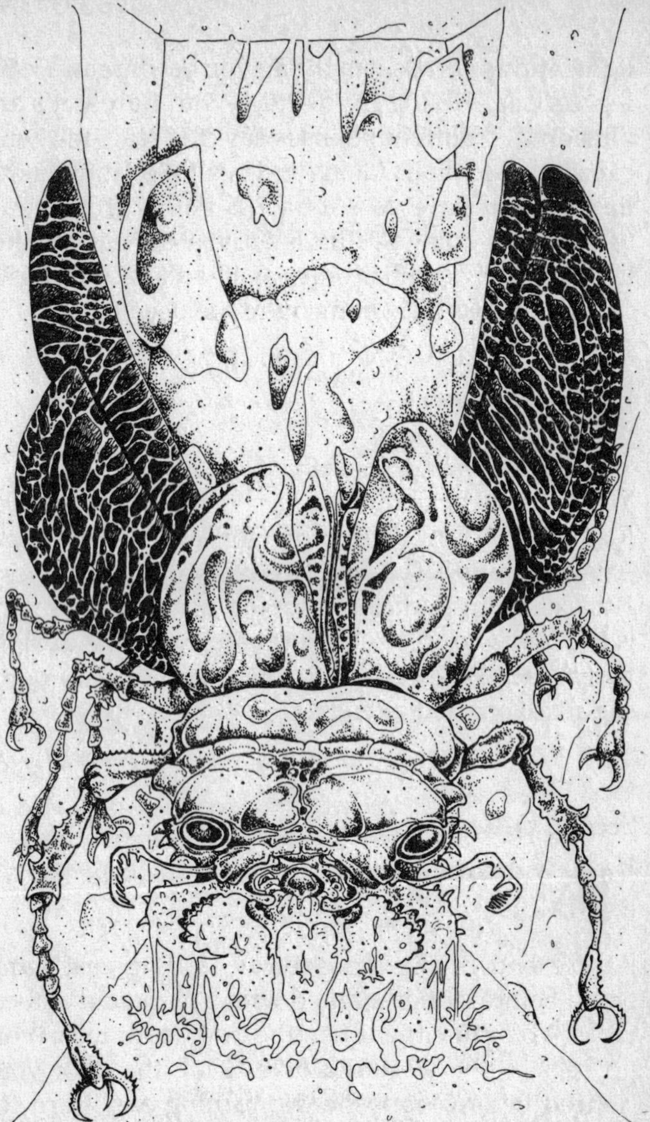

## 365

As you approach the dead end, the 'wall' at the end seems to evaporate away, forming into a large eight-legged yellow beetle with black wings and barbed jaws from which acid drips and hisses on the stone floor. The insect springs soundlessly forward at you before you can run. Do you have a silver medallion? If you do, turn to **170**. If you don't, turn to **389**.

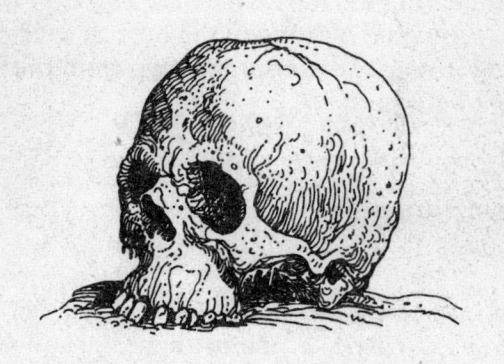

## 366

As you set foot in the chamber, the statue raises its right hand and grates out, 'Give me a gem.' Will you:

| | |
|---|---|
| Attack the statue? | Turn to **84** |
| Give the statue a gem, if you have one? | Turn to **8** |
| Do nothing for the moment? | Turn to **323** |
| Try to run past the statue to the stairs? | Turn to **340** |

## 367

You are confronted by a Dark Priest. You must fight for your life against this pitiless enemy, in this dark and terrible place!

DARK PRIEST      SKILL 9      STAMINA 13

If you win, turn to **117**.

## 368

You clamber into the nest. There are two eggs here, and you espy gold glinting in the nest as well – but mother Stormbird is swooping down from the sky! You must fight her.

GIANT STORMBIRD   SKILL 7   STAMINA 12

If you win, turn to **288**.

## 369

You cannot free the wizard, but at least you let him know you're a friend. You must fight the half-Ogre torturer; turn to **76**.

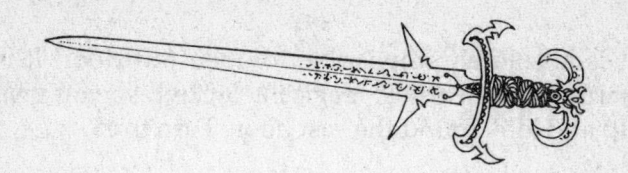

## 370
You hear the sound of snoring from behind the door to the east. You can either open it (turn to **107**) or open the south door instead (turn to **245**).

## 371
You cast your spell, and the spider shrinks back with a high-pitched, shrieking whine – but then it advances again; this illusion is so powerful that your spell has weakened it, but not destroyed it. You must now deal with it; turn to **175** and, if you must fight it, you may subtract 4 points of STAMINA from the spider's score thanks to the effects of your spell.

## 372
Choose the spell you're going to cast. Count up the number of letters in the name of the spell, and turn to the paragraph of that number. If a spell is described there, you will be safe; if not, ignore the paragraph you had turned to, and turn to **298** instead.

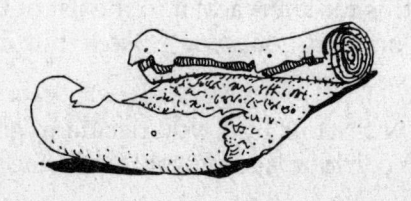

## 373

It is absolutely impossible to open this door! It is barred and clearly is magically locked, so you give up and look round the east door. Turn to **28**.

## 374

You open the box carefully, and inside you find a stoppered glass vial. The contents have long dried out, but there is some green residue left; after adding a little water, you have reconstituted a magical Potion of Healing! This will restore 4 STAMINA points when you drink it, which you can do at any time, except during combats. If you want to keep this for later, add it to the list of Equipment Carried on your *Adventure Sheet*, but cross it off when you do use it!

Pleased with your find, you decide to go back into the main corridor leading south and check the west wall for the secret door the man in the cell told you about; turn to **98**.

### 375
You push open the trapdoor and haul yourself up. You are in a dark room, and you can hear snoring close to you. Quietly, you tiptoe across the room, avoiding obstacles, towards a peacefully slumbering Orc. Taking no chances, you dispatch him with one swift blow as he sleeps. Turn to **99**.

### 376
You head back to the north, but when you enter the chamber you find it is filling with thick black smoke that is pouring from the stone face on the wall! The smoke is choking and deadly. Hastily shutting the door behind you, you go back south; you must enter the room at the end of the passageway. You can rush in with your sword in hand, ready to fight (turn to **25**), or you can enter without your weapon readied, trying a more peaceable approach (turn to **209**).

### 377
The door opens, revealing a passageway beyond; this ends at a T-junction. From here you can either go west (turn to **255**) or east (turn to **160**).

### 378
'Good,' says the lizard, 'so you won't have any trouble with the one that's left, will you?' There is no answer to this. Turn to **256**.

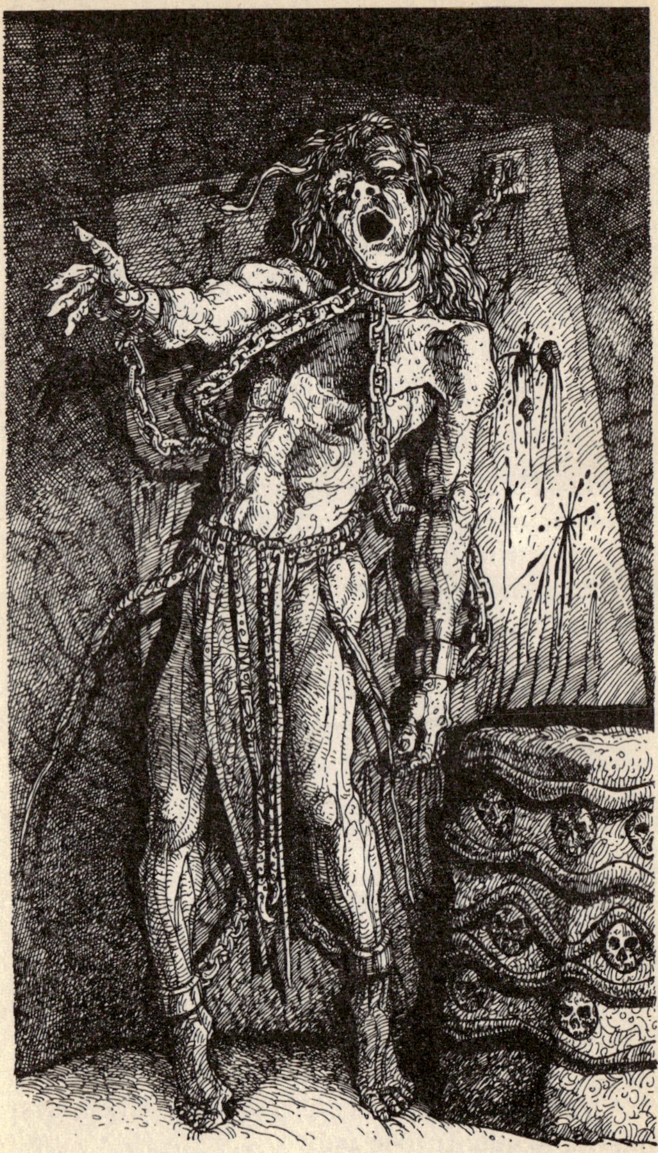

## 379

Struggling across rocky terrain, you arrive at the building just as twilight descends. This is a small, simple structure, without windows, but with an open door facing west. It is too gloomy to see what is inside. You will have to enter, for you need safe shelter, so you light a lantern and move in.

A groan greets you as you enter. In the gloom you make out a man chained to a wall, on one side of what could be an altar. He reaches out a hand to you as you enter and begs your help, mumbling in an unknown tongue. Will you:

| | |
|---|---|
| Attack him? | Turn to **69** |
| Approach and help him? | Turn to **390** |
| Stay where you are and look around you? | Turn to **37** |

## 380

You are now fighting the single Orc remaining, who curses your treachery!

ORC            SKILL 5            STAMINA 3

If you win, turn to **65**.

## 381

Now you may take the blue passageway (turn to 261) or the violet one (turn to 150).

## 382

You run blindly and blunder into a grey passage. You are running in fear, and you must deduct 1 point from your SKILL (this is *temporary*, and lasts until you have finished your next combat) and lose 2 STAMINA points. Turn to 112.

## 383

Mehrabian opens the door and drags out an old man, chained hand and foot. He is dirty, haggard and in pain, and below his eyes are dark circles of suffering. 'I won't talk,' he says weakly.

'Oh yes yer will, you ole bagger wind,' replies the half-Ogre, kicking the man to the ground. 'Gerrim up on the rack,' he tells you as he goes off to get a branding iron or two. You can either attack the half-Ogre (turn to 76) or help the old man (turn to 108).

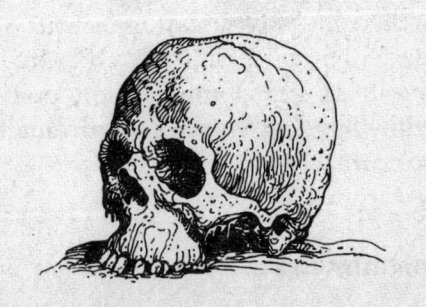

## 384

This set of steps is protected by some kind of magical force which slows your progress; it might have taken ages to reach the balcony but for your own 'Speed' spell! But Mordraneth will clearly have time to loose off one more spell before you can get to him. He scatters more dust into the air as he chants, and a Fire Globe comes streaking through the air at you! Are you wearing a Bronze Ring? If you are, turn to **231**. If you aren't, turn to **166**.

## 385

You enter a chamber which has a high, rocky ledge at the north end on which a bird sits, ripping at some bloodied mess (you can make out a human-like rib cage). The bird isn't very big, but its beak looks razor-sharp and is long, cruelly pointed, and stained with blood. It squawks and flies to attack you!

RAZORBEAK BIRD     SKILL 8     STAMINA 7

If you win, turn to **26**.

## 386

The Ebony Key slips into the lock and the door opens soundlessly, revealing a small room, featureless save for a sealed chest which stands on a central plinth. Do you want to enter this room and open the chest (turn to **293**) or leave it and head back east (turn to **114**)?

## 387

You move wearily along the corridor which terminates abruptly at a brown archway; beyond this you hear the sound of dripping water, and there is a foul stench here. Beyond the archway is a sewer – but there's nowhere else to go, so you wade into the scum and muck, and fight down your nausea. As you progress, you see glowing rainbow-coloured lights in the distance, and stride out to the welcome light; but you hear scrabbling sounds and squeaks that grow louder. Then the water seems to boil as a swarm of plague rats bursts forth and nips your legs and body! Will you:

| | |
|---|---|
| Cast a 'Speed' spell, if you can? | Turn to **23** |
| Cast a 'Dispel Illusion' spell, if you can? | Turn to **352** |
| Fight the rats? | Turn to **80** |
| Search in your backpack for something to use against the rats? | Turn to **48** |
| Run towards the light as fast as you can? | Turn to **251** |

### 388

At last your patient travels are rewarded. You turn a corner and, some fifty yards away, you see a pair of iron-railinged gates, set into limestone walls. You have reached your first goal – the entrance to the Iron Crypt! Turn to **277**.

### 389

Something in you senses that this creature is magical and unreal, but you'll still have to fight it!

BEETLE-ILLUSION     SKILL 5     STAMINA 6

Each time the Beetle-Illusion bites you, you must roll one die; on a roll of 1–3, take one *extra* point of damage to your STAMINA, from the acid on its jaws. If you win, turn to **115**.

### 390

As you move towards him, a sphere of deepest blackness flies from the fingers of his outstretched hand and engulfs you in a chilling circle of marrow-freezing cold as the illusion of his appearance vanishes. Deduct 6 STAMINA points. If you are still alive, the Dark Priest, armour-clad and mace-wielding, moves in for the kill. Turn to **367**.

### 391

This was a foolish waste of a spell; the 'Dispel Illusion' spell works against only illusory *creatures*, and has no effect here. Turn to **382**.

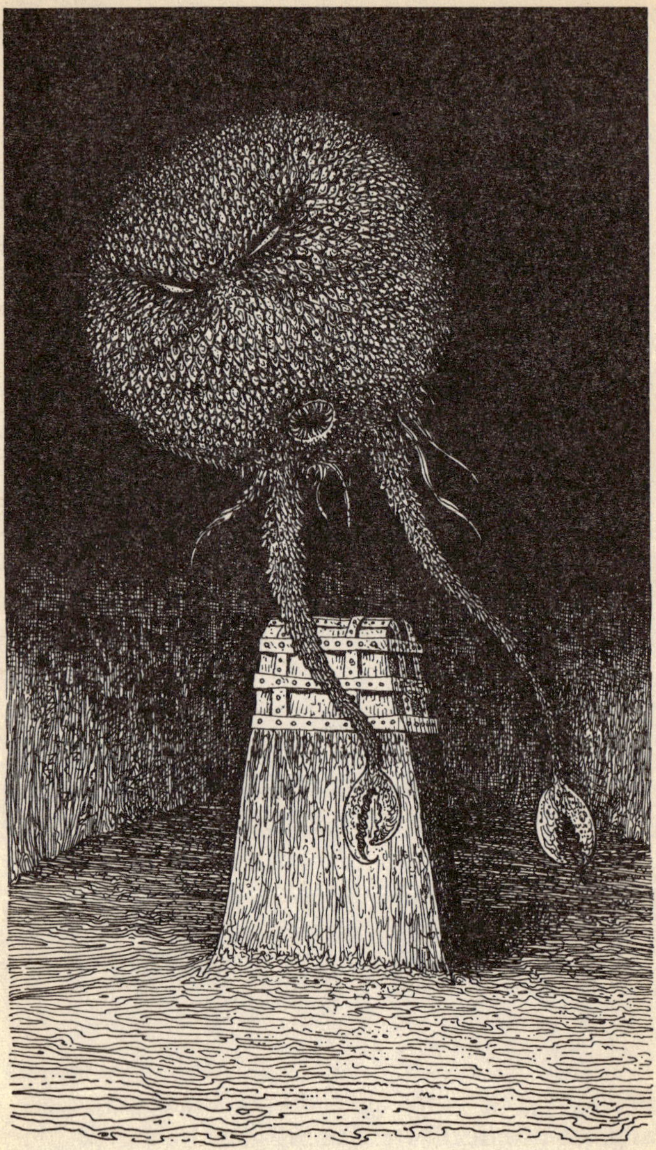

## 392

By your light source, you see that just beyond the doorway is a small alcove which opens into an almost circular room with a high domed ceiling. The walls are streaked with slime and mould, and the air is damp and stale. In the centre of the room, on a stone pedestal, is a chest made of rosewood, heavily banded and bound with black iron. The chest also has a guardian!

You glimpse an extraordinary creature flying towards you. Its body is a sphere of slimy grey-green scales, and two glowing, slitted red eyes glare at you. There is a small central fanged mouth on the sphere-body, but this is clearly not what the monster attacks with: it has two sharply clawed pincers that trail at the ends of two black-flecked green tentacles hanging below the body. The Diadrone is a strong guardian, and you will have to fight it; it flies too fast for you to escape.

DIADRONE    SKILL 8    STAMINA 12

If you win, turn to **12**.

## 393

You enter a well-lit room where an Orc is standing at a table, pouring oil into an intricate brass vessel of some kind. Around the table stand a few chairs, but there is no other decoration, save for a crude bunk bed. Two other doors lead south and east from this room.

The Orc snarls and draws his sword, and you must

fight him; but what *really* worries you is that as you enter he shouts, 'Master! Master!' . . .

ORC                SKILL 5             STAMINA 6

If you win, turn *immediately* to **202**, without taking any further actions *of any sort*! The Orc's master is about to arrive!

### 394

You are now fighting a Spider-Illusion, and if your sword is not a match for this dread creation, your adventure will end here!

SPIDER-ILLUSION      SKILL 8      STAMINA 12

If you win, turn to **269**.

### 395

You follow the green passage, and it takes on an increasingly blue tint, gradually shading to royal blue. The passage seems to go on for ever . . . 'You'll die of fatigue,' gloats the ghostly voice, 'or will your end be swifter?' Suddenly you hear the rush of water ahead of you, and a huge wave comes roaring down the passageway towards you! You turn to run, but the water smashes over you and knocks you, winded, to the ground. Water fills your lungs and your frantic efforts grow weak as you drown. Turn to **13**.

### 396

The walls compress and you stumble and fall; they close in on you, and you are being crushed to death. You feel ribs crack, and then you see the face of a dark-haired man radiating evil. He gloats: 'So powerful, the fear of enclosed spaces . . . an illusion which kills by trauma and shock . . . Farewell, foolish warrior. There will be none to stop me now.' Mordraneth's laughter is the last sound you will ever hear. Your quest ends here.

### 397

Do you have a silver medallion? If you do, turn to **95**. If you don't, turn to **230**.

### 398

The figure holds your head in its hands, and you feel energy pour into you. Regain 1 point of SKILL, 1 point of LUCK and 4 points of STAMINA; the LUCK point (and *only* the LUCK point) can take you above your *initial* LUCK score, if this applies here. But this effort drains the figure; slowly he fades away to nothingness. One of the other figures says softly, 'Now he is at peace. He has sacrificed his soul to give you strength to overcome the evil wizard. Do not fail his memory.' Filled with new hope, you press on. Will you:

| | |
|---|---|
| Take the yellow-green passage? | Turn to **307** |
| Take the azure passage? | Turn to **272** |
| Take the ochre passage? | Turn to **77** |

### 399

As you prod at the lid of the chest, a scything blade swings up from a crack in the stone floor – mercifully, on the side of chest opposite you! That was a close call! Now you may try to open the chest; turn to **246**.

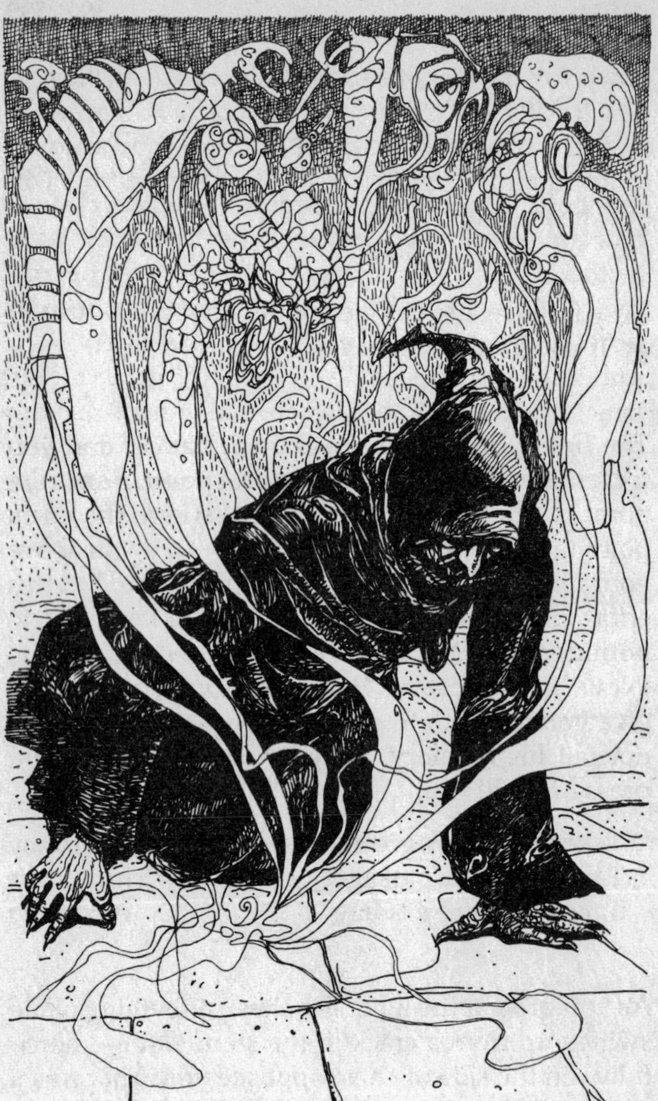

## 400

As Mordraneth falls at your feet, a great sigh is audible all round you, as if from hundreds of thousands of souls freed from a dreadful imprisonment of endless torment. Around you colours shimmer and grow pale, leaving only bare grey stone as the evil one's illusions decay and fade. Beyond the balcony, you now make out a passage, leading upwards to the fresh, clean air of the open world under the heavens, and you believe you can almost smell the sea. Perhaps Captain Garaeth will already be waiting to take you back to Pollua, to the glory and rewards you have so richly earned. Sheathing your sword for the last time, you stride upwards to find out.